5
INGREDIENT
INDIAN

5 INGREDIENT INDIAN

DELICIOUS RECIPES MADE EASY

CHETNA MAKAN

hamlyn

To my beautiful family.

First published in Great Britain in 2026 by Hamlyn,
an imprint of Octopus Publishing Group Ltd,
Carmelite House,
50 Victoria Embankment,
London EC4Y 0DZ
www.octopusbooks.co.uk

An Hachette UK Company
www.hachette.co.uk

The authorized representative in the EEA is
Hachette Ireland, 8 Castlecourt Centre, Dublin 15,
D15 XTP3, Ireland (email: info@hbgi.ie)

Distributed in the US by Hachette Book Group,
1290 Avenue of the Americas, 4th and 5th Floors,
New York, NY 10104

Distributed in Canada by Canadian Manda Group,
664 Annette St, Toronto, Ontario, Canada
M6S 2C8

ISBN: 978-0-600-63976-3
eISBN: 978-0-600-63977-0

A CIP catalogue record for this book
is available from the British Library.

Printed and bound in China.

10 9 8 7 6 5 4 3 2 1

Publisher: Kate Fox
Art Director: Juliette Norsworthy
Senior Editor: Leanne Bryan
Copy Editor: Emily Preece-Morrison
Photographer: Nassima Rothacker
Food Stylist: Maddie Rix
Props Stylist: Lauren Miller
Cover designer & Illustration: Jon Gray
 (gray318.com)
Production Manager: Caroline Alberti

MIX
Paper | Supporting
responsible forestry
FSC® C008047

CONTENTS

INTRODUCTION

Making Indian food accessible to everyone has been my driving force for the last few years. When I moved to the UK over 20 years ago, I was surprised to discover that many people still didn't know what we Indians ate day in, day out. I was often asked if I had naan and curry for dinner every day! Since then, things have definitely changed: people are more curious and ready to learn, and social media has opened more people's eyes to the real-life cooking of my homeland.

For the last ten years, I have been trying to simplify Indian home cooking for readers, one cookbook at a time. There are many amazing cookbooks out there, so I try to look for missing links and offer up something new each time. I have explored many subjects, from healthy Indian cookery to making more meals vegetarian, even cutting down the time it takes to cook Indian classics to 30 minutes. But this time, my thoughts went to one of the key issues people complain about when trying to make Indian food at home: the number of ingredients.

It's no secret that beginner or even some seasoned cooks perceive Indian cookery to include numerous ingredients, rafts of spices, pounding of pastes and slow-cooking to get those flavours we've come to love so well. But I'm here to tell you that it doesn't need to be that way. In all my books, I have always tried to simplify recipes, keeping them straightforward and accessible for the cook at home. This time, I am going a step further and cutting down the main ingredients to a mere five in total.

You might read this and wonder if that's truly possible. Surely, restricting yourself to five ingredients would mean compromising on flavour? But if you have made any of my recipes in the past you will know that flavour is not optional for me. How a dish looks is less of a concern, but tasting great is a non-negotiable. Every recipe in this book is on point in terms of flavour.

Of course, cooking an Indian dish with just five ingredients is not natural to the cuisine. We love our spices and every little spice brings a different note to a dish. Indeed, some Indians may find it difficult to accept this concept of ultimate simplicity! This book is about keeping ingredients to a minimum but delivering big on taste. I hope that even traditional Indian cooks will be tempted to give it a go and discover just how easy it can be to make a wonderful meal with minimal input.

To date, this has been my most challenging book to write. It took me a while to finalize the concept, because I wanted to do something that was not only useful but truly worked for every level of cooking ability. Everyone should be able to make a great-tasting Indian meal at home. Whether you are a student or someone who has been cooking for years, I want this book to be useful to one and all.

I have made sure that every recipe in the book brings something different. For example, each recipe in the chicken chapter (except for my Egg Curry) starts with the same base ingredient, but it was important to me that the end results are all completely unique. It took a lot of trials and testing, but I'm delighted that the flavour of every single dal is different, the taste of every flatbread is varied … and that has taken a lot of work in the kitchen. In addition, you will find a few *More Ways With* recipes dotted throughout the book where I suggest some alternatives to the recipe ingredients, to give you several different takes on the same recipe. I hope you will enjoy playing with the flavours to find your own favourite versions of each dish.

I have ensured that you can put a whole meal together from the recipes in this book. I begin with some snacks and starters, and move on to vegetable dishes (*sabji*), then there are lentil-based dishes, fish and chicken mains, and rice (*pulao*) and flatbreads to enjoy them with. Of course, there are also some essential accompaniments, including salads, raitas, my favourite chutneys, and not to forget some Indian sweets. You can create a feast with all the recipes here, and – yes – they are all made with just five ingredients each.

HOW IT WORKS

The five ingredients featured in each recipe will include the meat or veg, pulses or dairy, the spices (including my spice blends, see below) and the herbs. These you will have to intentionally go out and buy. But in addition to those five, there are naturally some storecupboard basics you will need to pull everything together. I cover these in detail on pages 10–11, but they include salt and pepper, oil or ghee for cooking, chilli powder and sugar. And that's it. If you feel like it, you can add your own garnishes, but I have left that entirely up to you.

MY SPICE BLENDS

The way that I bring as much flavour into the recipes as possible is through my spice blends (see pages 12–17). These are what we loosely call a 'masala', at home.

I have grown up with homemade masalas, prepared fresh every day. They're a vital part of how Indians cook at home and I prefer them to store-bought mixes. By keeping just five key spice blends in your storecupboard, you will have a whole world of flavour combinations to play with.

Keeping true to my concept, I have used just five ingredients to form each blend. Putting the blends together was like a jigsaw puzzle! Indian spice blends traditionally have a number of spices in them, with lots of different aromas and flavours coming together. To bring them down to just five components was not a simple task. But I was delighted by the results and I'm so excited for you to try them in these recipes.

Each spice blend recipe makes just a small quantity. Once you've tried them, it's easy to double the quantities next time. I have to be a realist – it's entirely possible to just go out and buy readymade versions of these spice blends to use in the recipes, but I would encourage you to try my blends at least once – you won't be disappointed!

I hope this book will find a forever home in your kitchen. My kids often commented, while tasting the recipes: 'Is it *really* just five ingredients, Mum?' I hope you too will be as pleasantly surprised when you cook these recipes, and – most importantly – enjoy eating them!

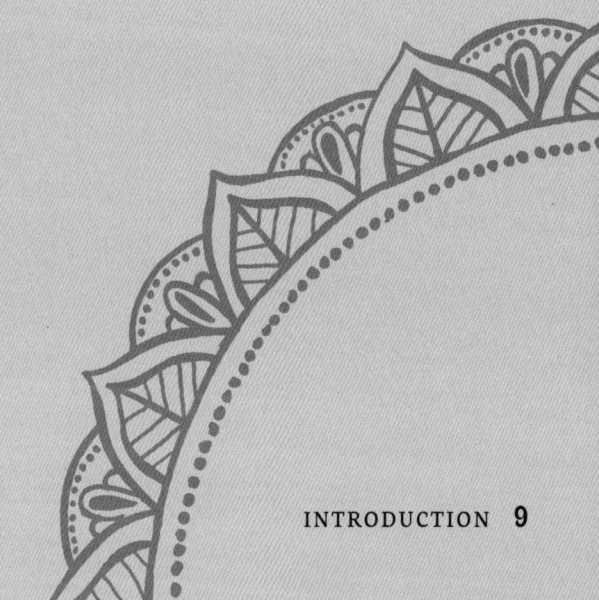

STORECUPBOARD BASICS

Whether you are new to cooking or a pro in the kitchen, this book should be quite straightforward to use. In addition to the five key ingredients of each recipe, there are five basic storecupboard ingredients you will need to have in stock to begin with. Keep these basics to hand and you can make any recipe in this book. You will not find them detailed in each ingredient list, but each method will tell you when to use them and how much to add.

1. Salt

Salt is the most basic ingredient that can make or break a dish. You can use table salt, sea salt, Himalayan salt, or any other variety you might use every day in your food. I use table salt in all my cooking. I do keep sea salt and other varieties in stock, but it's table salt that I go for when cooking Indian food. This is something I grew up with, but over the years I have noticed that every Indian kitchen seems to favour table salt for everyday cooking. You cannot go wrong there.

2. Pepper

You will notice that I don't really use too much pepper in my Indian cooking. It adds warmth and heat to dishes, but I don't find its flavour suitable for all dishes. I always keep ground black pepper and whole black peppercorns in the kitchen, and tend to use whole peppercorns more than ground. Regardless, it's a good spice to have as a staple in your cupboard.

3. Chilli Powder

This is the one spice that I receive the most questions about. For me, there was always just one chilli powder – the one that sat in my mum's spice box. It was red and adding it to a dish made it spicy. It was only when I moved to the UK that I realized things were not so straightforward. In essence, I want to say that chilli powder is ground red chillies – they can be hot and spicy or milder. In the UK, you can get different spice levels of chilli powder. They are always just pure ground chillies, but with differing levels of heat. In the US, 'chilli powder' is a spice mix of ground chillies, paprika and a few other spices that vary from brand to brand. It's a basic of Indian cookery, so this is one spice that is always good to have in the storecupboard.

4. Oil or Ghee

You'll need a fat of some kind to do any kind of cooking, whether it's a simple omelette or a fancy curry. Growing up, I watched my mum use sunflower oil or ghee (clarified butter) for nearly all her cooking. There was only one other option of mustard oil, which was only used for fish dishes and pickles. It was the same scenario in all the Indian kitchens I knew. Occasionally, I would spot a peanut oil, but that is all.

I used to incorporate a lot of sunflower oil in my everyday cooking, but have now moved to using rapeseed oil, because it is produced locally to where I live and I like the flavour it brings to food. I also use light olive oil, peanut oil and some butter. You can use whatever fat you prefer, just make sure it does not have a strong aroma or additional flavourings, as that will affect the taste of the dish. You can also feel free to mix a bit of oil and ghee in your dishes to make them taste even better.

Ghee has such a lovely flavour – a deep, smoky deliciousness. When cooking flatbreads, try making them with ghee instead of oil, as it adds a special crispness. And in rice-based dishes, the grains of rice become coated in the creaminess of the ghee.

5. Sugar

Whether you are cooking or baking, you will need some form of sugar in the kitchen. I have at least 6–8 types in stock at all times. The actual amount of sugar I use in Indian cooking is so minimal, it doesn't really matter which type you use. It could be caster sugar, golden caster sugar or light brown sugar, or even just white granulated sugar will work well, too.

A note on ginger and garlic paste:

Readymade ginger and garlic pastes, which you may have spotted in the Asian aisle of supermarkets, are not a storecupboard basic for everyone, yet are one of the five key ingredients in many of the recipes in the book. They are very handy and will save you time and effort. However, I find freshly made paste tastes much better and adds more punch to dishes. To make your own, peel and chop equal amounts of garlic and ginger, then blitz them together in a blender. Alternatively, just finely chop them together. Store in an airtight container in the refrigerator. It will keep well for a week.

SPICE BLENDS

Chaat masala

One of the classic sour and smoky spice blends, this is such a great masala to always have in your spice cupboard. The black salt (*kala namak*) adds a special tanginess to it. You can buy it in Asian supermarkets. Whether you're making salads, starters, soups, curries, rice or breads, this works with them all. I am never out of this spice blend – it's just the best.

20g (¾oz) cumin seeds
5g (⅛oz) peppercorns
10g (¼oz) ground ginger
15g (½oz) black salt (kala namak)
30g (1oz) mango powder (amchur)

Heat a frying pan over a low heat and dry-roast the cumin seeds for 2–3 minutes until fragrant and starting to change colour. Let them cool, then transfer to a spice grinder.

In the same pan, dry-roast the peppercorns for a couple of minutes until fragrant. Let them cool, then transfer to the spice grinder along with the ginger, salt and mango powder. Blend until you have a nice smooth powder.

Store in a clean, airtight jar in a cool, dark place for up to 6 months.

Tandoori masala

A vibrant, lively masala that is traditionally used on meats and vegetables to be cooked in the tandoor, an Indian oven. Here, I am keeping it light and fresh so you can use it in marinades, in curries or with yogurt dishes as well. The Kashmiri chilli powder brings a dash of colour without adding too much heat, but you can use a spicy chilli powder instead, if that is what you prefer.

4 tablespoons coriander seeds
seeds from 8 green cardamom pods
8 cloves
3 tablespoons Chaat Masala (see left)
2 tablespoons Kashmiri chilli powder

Heat a frying pan over a low heat and dry-roast the coriander seeds, cardamom seeds and cloves for 2–3 minutes until they start to change colour and become aromatic. Let cool, then transfer to a pestle and mortar or a spice grinder and crush to a powder.

Add the chaat masala and chilli powder to the mixture and mix well.

Store in a clean, airtight jar in a cool, dark place for up to 6 months.

CHAAT MASALA

SABJI MASALA

TANDOORI MASALA

PODI MASALA

GARAM MASALA

Sabji masala

This is the spice blend I use the most in everyday cooking. For me, it represents all the basic flavours I use in my food. From warming cumin to earthy coriander seeds, the roasting of which brings out the flavours from their cores. These, combined with the essential turmeric, some asafoetida for acidity and the sourness of mango powder, make it the most-used spice blend in my kitchen. I always have a big jar of this ready in my cupboard. You don't just have to use it for *sabjis*, it's great in lentils or rice or even snacks – a wonderful blend of spices.

50g (1¾oz) cumin seeds
50g (1¾oz) coriander seeds
50g (1¾oz) ground turmeric
5g (⅛oz) asafoetida
30g (1oz) mango powder (amchur)

Heat a frying pan over a low heat and dry-roast the cumin and coriander seeds for 5 minutes, stirring from time to time. Once they start to change colour and become aromatic, transfer to a pestle and mortar or spice grinder and crush to a fine powder.

Transfer to a bowl and add the turmeric, asafoetida and mango powder. Combine well.

Store in a clean, airtight jar in a cool, dark place for up to 6 months.

Garam masala

This is one of the most well-known spice mixes of Indian cuisine. Whether you have cooked Indian food before or not, you will surely have heard of garam masala, the spice blend that has travelled far and wide around the world. It is made with a mix of spices and every family has their own combination. I have used my mum's blend here.

10g (¼oz) cinnamon stick
5g (⅛oz) black cardamom pods
5g (⅛oz) green cardamom pods
20g (¾oz) cumin seeds
5g (1/8oz) cloves

First, crush the cinnamon and both types of cardamom (including the pods) in a pestle and mortar. This will break them up so they are easier to roast and grind to a powder.

Heat a frying pan over a low heat and dry-roast all the spices for 3–4 minutes, stirring frequently. Once they start to change colour and become smoky and aromatic, remove from the heat and let them cool completely.

Transfer everything to a spice grinder and grind to a fine powder.

Store in a clean, airtight jar in a cool, dark place for up to 6 months.

Podi masala

This is a great spice blend inspired by the South Indian *podi*, a powdered condiment of which there are many different varieties throughout the region. This blend is balanced and will add a bit of crunch as well as a savoury nutty flavour to your dishes. You can use it in dal and vegetable dishes, with rice or sprinkled over paratha. Stored in a jar in the refrigerator, it will last for a good couple of months.

200g (7oz) peanuts, skin-on
100g (3½oz) split yellow peas (chana dal)
1 tablespoon cumin seeds
6 garlic cloves, peeled
6 dried red chillies

Heat a frying pan over a low heat and dry-roast the peanuts for 8–10 minutes until aromatic and golden. Remove from the pan and set aside.

In the same pan, dry-roast the chana dal and cumin seeds over a low heat for 5–6 minutes until golden. Remove from the pan and set aside.

Next, in the same pan, dry-roast the garlic over a low heat for 5–6 minutes until golden. Remove from the pan and set aside.

Finally, heat 2 tablespoons oil in the same pan and roast the chillies for 1 minute over a low heat.

Transfer the chillies and garlic to a food processor. Add 1 teaspoon salt and blend until smooth, then add the rest of the roasted ingredients and blend to a coarse powder. Make sure not to over-blend, to avoid the peanut oils being released. Let cool completely before transferring to a clean jar.

Store in the refrigerator for up to 2 months.

SNACKS

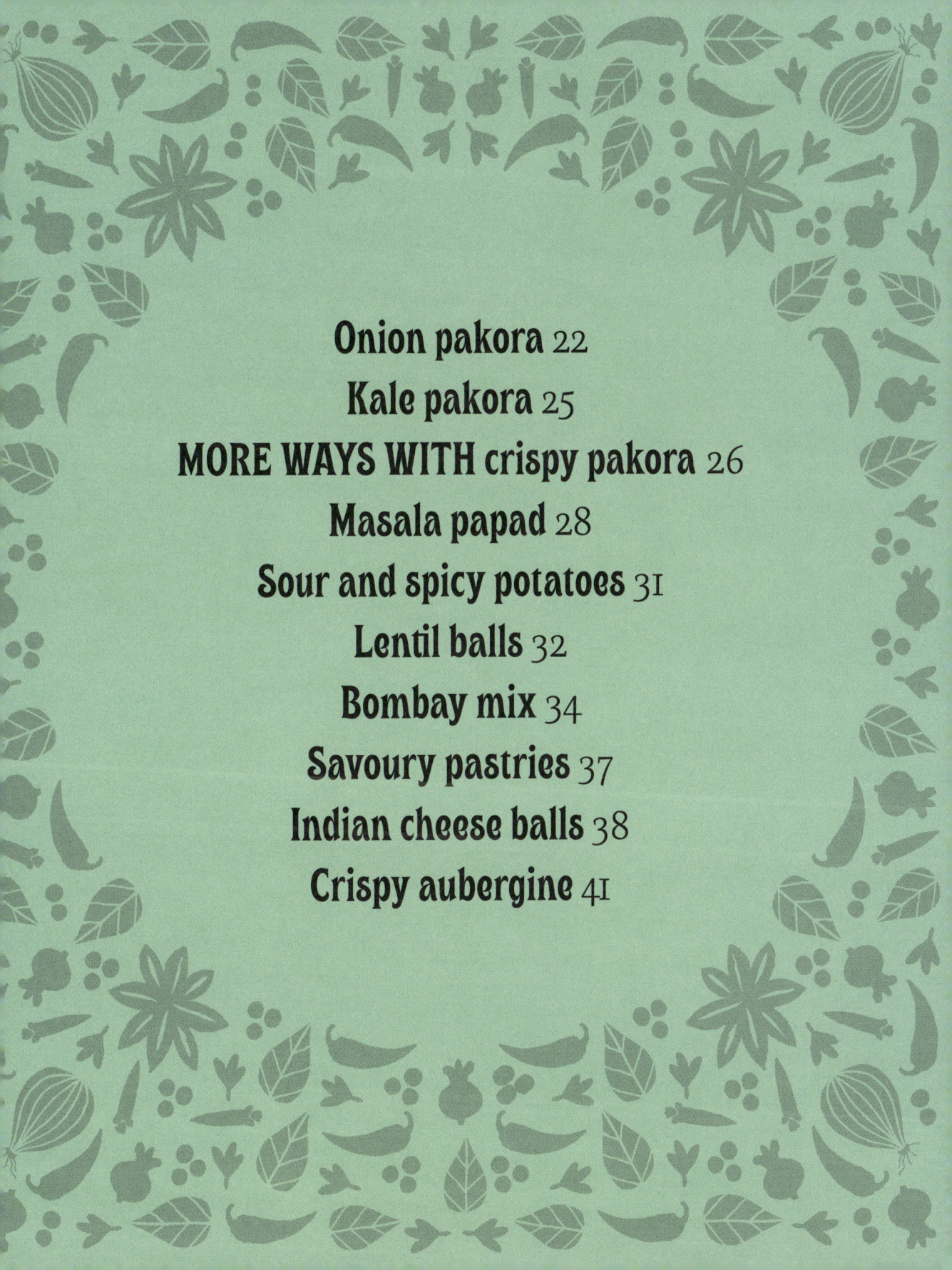

Onion pakora 22

Kale pakora 25

MORE WAYS WITH crispy pakora 26

Masala papad 28

Sour and spicy potatoes 31

Lentil balls 32

Bombay mix 34

Savoury pastries 37

Indian cheese balls 38

Crispy aubergine 41

The perfect snack that is ready in minutes, onion pakora is something that is mostly made when you have guests last minute or you want something quick with a cup of chai. Growing up in India, pakora were the most common snacks served by my mum and anyone else we visited. They're easy, delicious and perfect to eat while chatting with family and friends. Serve with some Coriander Chutney (see page 184). You can buy carom seeds in Asian supermarkets.

PYAAZ KA PAKORA

Onion pakora

SERVES 4

2 onions, thinly sliced

150g (5½oz) gram flour (besan)

1 teaspoon Chaat Masala (see page 13)

1 teaspoon carom seeds (ajwain)

handful of fresh coriander leaves, finely chopped

In a large mixing bowl, mix together all the ingredients with ½ teaspoon salt and 1 teaspoon chilli powder. Squash the onions to release a bit of moisture, then slowly add up to 100ml (3½fl oz) water to the mixture, stirring well to combine. You need just enough water to make the mixture sticky.

Heat enough oil for deep-frying in a deep-fat fryer or deep, heavy saucepan to 170°C (340°F), or until a cube of bread browns in 35 seconds. Add lime-sized portions of the onion batter to the hot oil and fry for 2–3 minutes until golden and crispy. Remove with a slotted spoon to drain on kitchen paper and serve hot.

These crispy, delightful little things are amazingly moreish and you might find it hard to stop at one. Serve with some Tamarind Chutney (see page 180) – a match made in heaven. If you don't have kale, you can use spinach leaves instead, but definitely try it with kale if you can.

Kale pakora

SERVES 4

150g (5½oz) gram flour (besan)

2 tablespoons rice flour

2 teaspoons Chaat Masala (see page 13)

1 teaspoon carom seeds (ajwain)

100g (3½oz) kale, cut into 5-cm (2-inch) pieces

In a large mixing bowl, mix together the flours along with ½ teaspoon salt, ½ teaspoon chilli powder, 1 teaspoon of the chaat masala and the carom seeds. Add 200ml (7fl oz) water and mix to a batter of the same consistency as a pancake batter.

Heat enough oil for deep-frying in a deep-fat fryer or deep, heavy saucepan to 160–170°C (320–340°F), or until a cube of bread browns in 35–40 seconds.

Dip the kale leaves into the batter and fry them in the hot oil until golden and crispy. Remove with a slotted spoon to drain on kitchen paper.

Sprinkle with the rest of the chaat masala and serve hot.

MORE
WAYS
WITH

CRISPY PAKORA

This pakora batter is really versatile and can be used with almost any vegetable. Here are a couple of my favourite pakora. You can experiment with any seed spices or leafy vegetables here.

To make **spinach pakora**, replace the kale with 100g (3½oz) baby spinach leaves. You could also substitute the carom seeds (*ajwain*) for cumin seeds, if you prefer.

To make **fenugreek pakora**, replace the kale with 100g (3½oz) roughly chopped fenugreek leaves and the carom seeds with 1 tablespoon grated fresh root ginger. Reduce the amount of water in the batter to 100ml (3½fl oz). Fry the battered leaves in clumps until golden and crispy. You might not think of fenugreek leaves as being a primary ingredient for pakora, but it's a common Maharashtrian recipe for a quick and easy lunch. They go particularly well with a little Coconut Chutney (see page 181), too.

Before moving to the UK, I didn't know these could be served as starters, which I found interesting. To me, *papad* were an accompaniment to a meal or served as a snack. Some meals, such as dal rice or *kadhi* rice, were not complete without these served on the side. Once you add the masala to the *papad*, it becomes a fantastic snack to have with drinks or some chai, but you have to make sure to eat it straight away before it gets soggy.

Masala papad

SERVES 4

1 red onion, finely chopped

1 tomato, finely chopped

½ teaspoon Chaat Masala (see page 13)

4 cooked papad (poppadoms)

handful of sev (gram-flour noodles)

In a medium bowl, mix together the onion, tomato and chaat masala with ¼ teaspoon salt and ¼ teaspoon chilli powder.

Place the papads on serving plates and sprinkle the onion masala on top. Sprinkle with some sev and eat immediately.

This is a great snack to serve with some chai or drinks, and also makes a great side to some dal and roti. Leftovers work perfectly in a wrap or sandwich, making it a great little recipe. You can even substitute sweet potatoes for the potatoes.

CHATPATA ALU

Sour and spicy potatoes

SERVES 4

4 potatoes, peeled and cut into 1-cm (½-inch) batons

1 teaspoon cumin seeds

1 teaspoon black mustard seeds

1 tablespoon Sabji Masala (see page 16)

2 teaspoons Chaat Masala (see page 13)

Put the potatoes in a pan and cover with water. Bring to the boil and cook for 4 minutes, then drain immediately.

Heat 4 tablespoons oil in a large, deep frying pan, then add the cumin and mustard seeds. Once they start to sizzle, reduce the heat and stir in the sabji masala and chaat masala along with 1 teaspoon salt, 1 teaspoon chilli powder and then 50ml (2fl oz) water.

Add the potatoes to the pan and cook over a medium–high heat for 8–10 minutes until the potatoes are cooked through and crispy on the edges. Serve.

These are always a winner when cooking for family and friends. So simple, crispy and moreish, I often make them for get-togethers or a weekend snack. Serve with some Coriander or Tamarind Chutney (see page 184 or 180).

DAL VADA
Lentil balls

SERVES 4

300g (10½oz) urid dal (split skinless black lentils)

1 onion, finely chopped

handful of fresh coriander, finely chopped

2.5-cm (1-inch) piece of fresh root ginger, peeled and finely chopped

1 teaspoon Chaat Masala (see page 13)

Soak the dal in water for 2–3 hours or overnight. Drain, then blitz to a coarse paste. Add the onion, coriander, ginger and chaat masala to the paste along with 1 teaspoon salt and 1 teaspoon chilli powder. Combine well.

Heat enough oil for deep-frying in a deep-fat fryer or deep, heavy saucepan to 170°C (340°F), or until a cube of bread browns in 35 seconds. Carefully add walnut-sized portions of the batter to the hot oil and fry for a couple of minutes until golden and crispy. Remove with a slotted spoon to drain on kitchen paper and serve.

'Bombay mix' is a term I first heard when I came to the UK and was quite surprised by it. In India, we call this *namkeen* and there are hundreds if not thousands of variations on it. Every region, every town, every city has its own special *namkeen*. This one is my favourite because I grew up eating it, it's something my mum has made forever and continues to do so today. This will keep in a sealed jar for a good month, if not eaten before that!

NAMKEEN

Bombay mix

SERVES 6–8

150g (5½oz) peanuts, skin on

150g (5½oz) poha (flattened rice)

40–50 fresh curry leaves

10 green chillies, split in half

1 teaspoon ground turmeric

Heat enough oil for deep-frying in a deep-fat fryer or deep, heavy saucepan to 160–170°C (320–340°F), or until a cube of bread browns in 35–40 seconds.

Fry the skin-on peanuts in batches until golden. Remove with a slotted spoon to drain on kitchen paper, then place in a large bowl.

In the same oil, fry the poha in batches for a few seconds until it puffs up and becomes crispy. This takes no time at all, so make sure to remove from the oil quickly or else it will burn. Transfer to the bowl with the peanuts.

In the same way, working in batches, fry the curry leaves and green chillies for a minute until crisped up, then add to the bowl.

While everything is still hot, add the turmeric to the bowl along with 1 teaspoon salt, 1 teaspoon chilli powder and ½ teaspoon sugar. Mix well and let cool completely before serving.

This is such an easy snack that will make you smile every time you eat it. The pasty is short and light, with flavours of carom seeds (*ajwain*) and fenugreek. You can shape them into circles or cut them into strips, or any other shape you like, as long as it's nice and thin. Enjoy as a snack or make a *chaat* (a savoury snack of potatoes, chickpeas, yogurt and chutneys) with them or serve with dips, such as Coriander Chutney (see page 184).

PAPDI
Savoury pastries

SERVES 6–8

300g (10½oz) plain flour

½ teaspoon carom seeds (ajwain)

1 tablespoon dried fenugreek leaves (kasuri methi)

Put the flour in a bowl along with the carom seeds, dried fenugreek leaves, ¾ teaspoon salt, ½ teaspoon chilli powder and ½ teaspoon sugar. Mix well. Add 3 tablespoons oil and mix until it has the texture of breadcrumbs. Slowly add 140ml (4½fl oz) water and bring it to a soft dough. You might not need all the water or may need a bit more, so add a little at a time. Cover and leave to rest for 30 minutes.

Split the dough into small grape-sized balls and roll each into a very thin disc, roughly 1–2mm (1/16 inch) thick. Prick all over with a knife or a fork.

Heat enough oil for deep-frying in a deep-fat fryer or deep, heavy saucepan to 160–170°C (320–340°F), or until a cube of bread browns in 35–40 seconds. Fry the papdi in batches for 3–4 minutes until golden and crispy. Remove with a slotted spoon to drain on kitchen paper and leave to cool.

Serve when cool. You can store them in an airtight jar for 3–4 weeks, that is if they don't get eaten before then!

This is one snack I always end up making for get-togethers and parties. Although my friends are used to seeing it on my menu, they still love it and enjoy it as if having it for the first time. *Vada* are perfect party food or great for a snack at family dinners. The good thing is that they taste as amazing at room temperature as they do piping hot, so are the ideal thing to prepare before your guests arrive. Serve with Coriander Chutney (see page 184) for the full flavour explosion.

PANEER VADA

Indian cheese balls

MAKES 20

225g (8oz) paneer, grated

2 medium potatoes, peeled, boiled and mashed

1½ teaspoons Chaat Masala (see page 13)

handful of fresh coriander leaves, finely chopped

2 tablespoons cornflour

Mix all the ingredients in a large bowl, along with ¾ teaspoon salt and 1 teaspoon chilli powder. Divide into 20 small portions.

Heat enough oil for deep-frying in a deep-fat fryer or deep, heavy saucepan to 170°C (340°F), or until a cube of bread browns in 35 seconds. Fry the balls in batches for a couple of minutes until crispy and golden all over. Remove with a slotted spoon to drain on kitchen paper.

I love how the humble aubergine can be cooked in such different ways, all resulting in different flavours, whether you roast it for *bharta*, cook it in some rice or curry, or fry it in pakora. This crispy aubergine is a bit different. Covered in spices that permeate the flesh, the slices are then given a crispy finish with semolina. They make a great snack. The chutney is optional – you can serve them with ketchup or mayo as well, but I like to eat them just as they are.

KARARA BAIGAN
Crispy aubergine

SERVES 4

1 large aubergine

1 tablespoon Sabji Masala (see page 16)

150g (5½oz) semolina

1 teaspoon Chaat Masala (see page 13)

Coriander Chutney (see page 184), to serve (optional)

Slice the aubergine into thin discs, each about 5mm (¼ inch) thick.

In a small bowl, mix ¾ teaspoon salt and 1 teaspoon chilli powder with the sabji masala. Sprinkle the spice mix on both side of the aubergine slices and leave to sit for 10–15 minutes. This will release the moisture from the aubergine and allow time for the flesh to absorb the spices.

In a separate bowl, mix the semolina with the chaat masala. Roll the aubergine slices in the semolina mixture, making sure you coat them well.

Heat enough oil for shallow-frying in a large frying pan and fry the slices for 2–3 minutes on each side until golden and crispy.

Drizzle some chutney on top, if you like, and serve.

VEG

Okra is often unfairly criticised for being slimy and sticky, but cooked well it's a delicious ingredient. Wash and dry it well before cutting, to prevent it becoming soggy, then ensure you cook it for enough time to remove any sliminess – do not stop cooking until you are sure you've reached that point. Taste a little to check when you are close to the end of the cooking time. This simple yet effective way of cooking okra will make you fall in love with it.

PYAAZ BHINDI
Onion okra sabji

SERVES 4

1 teaspoon cumin seeds

1 onion, thinly sliced

500g (1lb 2oz) okra, washed and dried well

1 tablespoon Sabji Masala (see page 16)

1 tablespoon lemon juice

Heat 3 tablespoons oil of your choice in a frying pan. Add the cumin seeds and let them sizzle for a few seconds before adding the onion. Cook over a medium heat for 2 minutes until starting to soften.

Top and the tail the okra and cut into 1-cm (½-inch) pieces. Add these to the pan and cook for 20 minutes over a low–medium heat, stirring every 5 minutes, until any sliminess has disappeared.

Add the sabji masala along with 1 teaspoon salt and 1 teaspoon chilli powder and mix well. Cook over a high heat for 2 minutes before adding the lemon juice. Mix well, then serve.

A staple in Indian kitchens, cauliflower *sabji* is made all over India, with differing spices used in each region. I love making this to serve with dal and rice. Leftover *sabji* serves as the perfect filling for a lunch wrap with some ketchup and mayo.

GOBHI SABJI
Cauliflower sabji

SERVES 4

1 teaspoon cumin seeds

2 onions, thinly sliced

2 tablespoons ginger and garlic paste

1 tablespoon Sabji Masala (see page 16)

1 cauliflower, cut into small florets

Heat 2 tablespoons oil of your choice in a saucepan. Add the cumin seeds, then after a few seconds of sizzling, add the onions. Cook over a low–medium heat for 5 minutes until the onions have softened.

Add the ginger and garlic paste and cook for 2 minutes, then add 1 teaspoon salt, 1 teaspoon chilli powder and the sabji masala. Mix well.

Add the cauliflower florets along with 2 tablespoons water. Mix well, then cover and cook over a low–medium heat for 15 minutes until the cauliflower is cooked.

Uncover and cook over a high heat for a final 2 minutes to evaporate any remaining moisture and crisp up some edges. Serve.

This *sabji* is one of my absolute favourite ways to eat fenugreek. The ginger is all you need in the way of extra flavour, as the fenugreek is so strong and delicious you don't need anything else. If you ever spot fresh fenugreek leaves in an Asian shop, you must buy them and try this recipe. The fresh leaves keep in the refrigerator for 3–4 days and the leaves can also be picked and then frozen for future use. Enjoy with some Carom Seed Flatbreads (see page 170) or plain roti (see page 159).

METHI ALU

Fenugreek potato

SERVES 4

200g (7oz) fresh fenugreek leaves

2 potatoes, peeled and cut into 1-cm (½-inch) pieces

2.5-cm (1-inch) piece of fresh root ginger, peeled and finely chopped

Heat 2 tablespoons oil in a large, deep frying pan over a low heat. Add the fenugreek leaves, potatoes and ginger along with 1 teaspoon salt and 1 teaspoon chilli powder. Mix well, then cover and cook for 10–15 minutes until the potatoes are cooked through.

Uncover and cook over a high heat for a final 2 minutes to evaporate any remaining moisture, then serve.

Tasting so smoky and delicious, this aubergine dish pairs perfectly with some plain roti (see page 159) or hot Carom Seed Flatbreads (see page 170). It's not just good as a main meal – it also works as a chutney or dip with some crisps on the side and makes a great partner for some dal rice.

BAIGAN BHARTA
Smoked aubergine

SERVES 4

2 aubergines

2 onions, roughly chopped

1 tablespoon ginger and garlic paste

2 tablespoons tomato purée

1 tablespoon Sabji Masala (see page 16)

Preheat the grill to high.

Brush a drop of oil all over the aubergines. Prick the skin all over with a sharp knife, then cook under the hot grill for 30 minutes, turning half way through. The aubergines should be soft and mushy.

Heat 2 tablespoons oil in a large, deep frying pan over a low heat, add the onions and cook for 6–8 minutes until lightly golden. Add the ginger and garlic paste and cook for another minute, then add the tomato purée and cook for 5 minutes. Now add ½ teaspoon salt, ½ teaspoon chilli powder and the sabji masala. Mix well.

Peel the aubergines and chop up the insides before adding to the pan. Cook over a medium heat for 5 minutes, then serve.

Fresh seasonal veg hits differently and doesn't need much at all to make it sing. I add some onions here for slightly more texture and flavour, but you can make this even without the onions. Finishing it with lemon juice keeps it fresh and zingy. Enjoy this with any *pulao* or some paratha (see pages 160–70), or put it on some toast for a snack.

Asparagus sabji

SERVES 4

2 onions, thinly sliced

400g (14oz) asparagus stalks, cut in half

1 teaspoon Chaat Masala (see page 13)

1 tablespoon lemon juice

Heat 2 tablespoons oil in a large, deep frying pan and add the onions. Cook over a low heat for 5–6 minutes until they are softened and starting to change colour.

Add the asparagus and stir-fry for 5 minutes or so until they start to get charred.

Add ¼ teaspoon salt, ½ teaspoon chilli powder along with the chaat masala and mix well. Drizzle the lemon juice on top and serve.

Growing up, I was never a fan of *karela* (bitter gourd), but I fell in love with this unique vegetable as I got older and understood that its bitterness is just so delicious along with spices. Now, I always make a big batch of this *sabji* and eat it as a condiment with my meals. It keeps well in the refrigerator for a good week and goes perfectly with dal rice or just some paratha (see pages 160–70).

KARELA
Bitter gourd

SERVES 4

8 bitter gourds (karela)

2 onions, thinly sliced

1 tablespoon Sabji Masala (see page 16)

1½ teaspoons mango powder (amchur)

Peel off the chunkier bits of gourd skin (you don't have to cut away all of it), then cut the gourds into 5-mm (¼-inch) discs. Sprinkle with 1 teaspoon of salt and set aside for 1 hour. After this time, wash the pieces and pat dry.

Heat enough oil for shallow frying in a large, deep frying pan and fry the gourd pieces in batches until lightly golden. Remove from the pan and set aside.

Reduce the oil in the pan to just 2 tablespoons and add the onions. Cook over a medium heat for 5 minutes until softened and just beginning to colour. Add the gourd pieces back to the pan and cook for 15 minutes over a low heat.

Now add ½ teaspoon salt and ½ teaspoon chilli powder along with sabji masala and mango powder and mix well. Cook for a final 2 minutes, then serve.

Cabbage might be something you think of for making coleslaw, but it comes to life when made into a *sabji* with just a few basic spices. The fresh ginger and coriander add another layer to this very delicious stir-fry. Serve with plain roti (see page 159) or Carom Seed Flatbreads (see page 170) or on the side of dal and rice. It's great as a sandwich or wrap filling, too.

PATTA GOBHI SABJI
Cabbage sabji

SERVES 4

1 teaspoon black mustard seeds

1 white or green cabbage, thinly sliced

2 tablespoons finely chopped fresh root ginger

1 teaspoon Chaat Masala (see page 13)

handful of fresh coriander, finely chopped

Heat 2 tablespoons oil in a large, deep frying pan and add the mustard seeds. Once they start to pop, add the cabbage and ginger and cook over a high heat for 4–5 minutes, stirring often, then reduce the heat and cook for 20 minutes until the cabbage is soft.

Add ½ teaspoon salt and ½ teaspoon chilli powder along with the chaat masala and the chopped coriander. Mix it all well and serve.

This green stir-fry is inspired by South Indian *poriyal*, which is a Tamil word for stir-fry. I have obviously reduced the number of ingredients from the classic dish and given it a simpler finish, keeping the flavours alive. It's a must-try, delicious, healthy dish to enjoy with some roti (see page 159) or paratha (see pages 160–70). Tinned coconut meat can be found in Asian supermarkets.

PHALIYAAN PORIYAL

Green bean stir-fry

SERVES 4

100g (3½oz) fresh coconut meat

1 teaspoon black mustard seeds

10–15 fresh curry leaves

200g (7oz) fine green beans, each cut in half

3 tablespoons Podi Masala (see page 17)

In a blender, blitz the fresh coconut meat until it's nice and coarse.

Heat 2 tablespoons oil in a large, deep frying pan. Add the mustard seeds and curry leaves and let them sizzle over a low heat. Now add the beans, coconut and podi masala along with 2 tablespoons water. Cover and cook for 10 minutes, then serve.

This is one of those dishes I make without even thinking. I always have a block or two of paneer in the refrigerator as it makes for such quick meals and adds textures to other dishes. The base of onions and tomatoes is perfect for this *bhurji*, which translates to 'scrambled' in English. Eat with some plain roti (see page 159) or paratha (see pages 160–70), or even a slice of toast will be perfect.

PANEER BHURJI
Scrambled Indian cheese

SERVES 4

1 teaspoon black mustard seeds

4 onions, roughly chopped

2 tomatoes, roughly chopped

1 tablespoon Sabji Masala (see page 16)

450g (1lb) paneer, crumbled

Heat 2 tablespoons oil in a large, deep frying pan and add the mustard seeds. Once they start to pop, add the onions and cook over a medium-low heat for 8 minutes until golden.

Add the tomatoes along with 2 tablespoons water, cover and cook for 10 minutes over a low heat until the tomatoes have softened.

Add ½ teaspoon salt and 1 teaspoon chilli powder along with the sabji masala, then add the paneer. You can crumble the paneer or grate it or even cut into tiny pieces. Mix it all well and cook for a final 5 minutes over a low–medium heat, then serve.

MORE
WAYS
WITH

BHURJI

A *bhurji* is a type of 'scramble', similar to scrambled eggs but cooked with onions and tomatoes, which Indians traditionally eat scooped up with some paratha or roti. I often enjoy it on toast. It's a simple, adaptable dish, designed to be whipped up in a moment, and you can play around with the ingredients and spicing. Paneer and mustard seeds are my favourite combo, but eggs are an obvious, delicious variation, while tofu also lends itself well to scrambling.

To make an **egg bhurji** couldn't be easier: 6 lightly whisked eggs, scrambled and lightly cooked for a minute or two before serving, along with a handful of finely chopped fresh coriander. You can leave out the mustard seeds. The silky eggs combined with tomato sauce make an ideal breakfast dish.

For a **tofu bhurji**, simply swap the mustard seeds for cumin seeds and the paneer for a 400g (14oz) block of firm tofu, crumbled or cut into small pieces.

DAL & MORE

Whole black lentils 70

Split yellow lentils 73

Whole brown lentils 75

Spinach lentils 76

Red kidney beans 79

MORE WAYS WITH bean curry 80

Podi chickpeas 82

Potato curry 85

Split mung beans 86

Spinach and Indian cheese 88

One of our family favourites, I always make double quantities so that we can have a few meals of this. It's so creamy, warming and wholesome that you will want to make it on all special occasions. Serve with naan, paratha (see pages 160–70) or a simple *pulao*.

KAALI DAL
Whole black lentils

SERVES 4

350g (12oz) urid beans (whole black lentils)

2 tablespoons ginger and garlic paste

2 tablespoons tomato purée

1 tablespoon Garam Masala (see page 16)

4 tablespoons double cream

Place the beans in a large saucepan and add 2 litres (3½ pints) water. Leave to soak for 2 hours. This will help them cook more quickly, but you can skip the soaking if you don't have time. You might think this is a lot of water, but you will need this much or a bit more to cook the dal for a long time.

Add 2 teaspoons salt to the water and bring to the boil, then reduce the heat and simmer for 1½ hours, or until the lentils are cooked, soft and starting to disintegrate.

Heat 4 tablespoons ghee or oil of your choice in a separate small pan. Add the ginger and garlic paste and reduce the heat to low. Cook for 1 minute, then add the tomato purée along with 100ml (3½fl oz) water and cook for 5 minutes. Stir in the garam masala.

Add the spice paste to the cooked dal and mix well. If you need more water, now is a good time to add 200ml (7fl oz) or so of boiling water. Cover and cook the dal for a further 30 minutes over a low heat until it becomes creamy and thick.

Finally, add the cream and mix well, then serve.

Chana dal is one of the creamiest lentils – it doesn't require additional cream adding to it. It takes longer than other lentils to cook, but when cooked properly it starts to disintegrate and become thick and velvety, which makes it stand out from other lentils. Here, it's cooked with just some garlic and earthy dill, which lift it to the next level. Enjoy with Carom Seed Flatbreads (see page 170) or any other flatbreads.

CHANA DAL
Split yellow lentils

SERVES 4

300g (10½oz) split yellow peas (chana dal)

1 teaspoon ground turmeric

1 teaspoon cumin seeds

6–8 garlic cloves, thinly sliced

handful of fresh dill, finely chopped

Place the dal in a large saucepan and add 2 litres (3½ pints) water. Leave to soak for 2 hours. This will help the dal cook more quickly, but you can skip the soaking if you don't have time.

Add I teaspoon salt along with the turmeric to the water and bring to the boil, then reduce the heat and simmer for I–I½ hours until the dal is cooked, soft and starting to disintegrate.

Heat 3 tablespoons ghee or oil of your choice in a separate small pan. Add the cumin seeds. Once they start to sizzle, add the garlic and turn the heat off as soon as the garlic starts to change colour. Add I teaspoon chilli powder then pour the mixture over the cooked dal. Sprinkle with the dill, then serve.

There is such an earthy flavour to this dal, which sets it apart from others, teamed with tomatoes, which round it off beautifully. It doesn't take long to cook either. Enjoy with plain roti (see page 159), paratha (see pages 160–70) or any *pulao*, or just plain rice.

SABUT MASOOR DAL
Whole brown lentils

SERVES 4

300g (10½oz) brown lentils (sabut masoor dal)

1 teaspoon cumin seeds

2 tomatoes, finely chopped

1 tablespoon Sabji Masala (see page 16)

1 teaspoon mango powder (amchur)

Put the lentils in a saucepan along with 1.5 litres (2¾ pints) water and 1 teaspoon salt and bring to the boil. Reduce the heat to medium–low and simmer for 25–30 minutes until the lentils are soft and starting to break up and become mushy.

Heat 3 tablespoons ghee or oil of your choice in a separate small pan. Add the cumin seeds. Once they start to sizzle, add the tomatoes and cook for 6–8 minutes until soft. Add the sabji masala, mango powder and 1 teaspoon chilli powder. Mix well, then pour over the lentils and serve.

This is one of my favourite ways of cooking dal. The addition of spinach to the already healthy lentils makes it even more nutritious – it's a great one-pot meal. You can serve this with plain roti (see page 159) or some rice. It is also great as a soup, with a slice of sourdough or garlic bread.

PALAK DAL

Spinach lentils

SERVES 4

300g (10½oz) split red lentils (masoor dal)

1 teaspoon ground turmeric

200g (7oz) spinach leaves, roughly chopped

1 teaspoon cumin seeds

6–8 garlic cloves, thinly sliced

Put the lentils in a saucepan and add 1.2 litres (2 pints) water, 1 teaspoon salt and the ground turmeric. Bring to the boil, then reduce the heat to low and simmer for 10 minutes until the lentils are soft and starting to break apart.

Add the spinach and cook for 5 minutes over a low heat until wilted.

Heat 4 tablespoons of ghee or oil of your choice in a separate small pan and add the cumin seeds. Once they start to sizzle, add the garlic and cook over a low heat for 1 minute until it starts to change colour. Add 1 teaspoon chilli powder, then pour the mixture over the cooked dal. Mix well and serve.

Being Punjabi, *rajma* (red kidney bean curry) will always be special to me. Growing up, we would eat this with crispy Carom Seed Flatbreads (see page 170) and the combination of these two dishes is magical, to put it simply. This also goes very well with some plain fluffy rice. Add some Crunchy Salad (see page 195) for more joy.

RAJMA

Red kidney beans

SERVES 4

2 teaspoons cumin seeds

3 onions, roughly chopped

2 tablespoons ginger and garlic paste

1 tablespoon Sabji Masala (see page 16)

2 × 400g (14oz) cans of red kidney beans, drained and rinsed

Heat 2 tablespoons oil in a saucepan and add the cumin seeds. Once they start to sizzle, add the onions and cook over a medium heat for 8–10 minutes until deeply golden. Add the ginger and garlic paste and cook for another minute.

Add the sabji masala along with 1 teaspoon salt and 1 teaspoon chilli powder. Mix well, then add the kidney beans along with 200ml (7fl oz) water. Bring to the boil, then cover and cook over a low heat for 15 minutes.

After this time, you can turn off the heat and let it sit for 30 minutes to let the beans soak up the flavours, or serve immediately – it all depends on how hungry you are!

MORE
WAYS
WITH

BEAN CURRY

Rajma (kidney bean curry) is a wholesome, soothing dish that hails from the Punjab, and is packed with protein and fibre. The traditional long, slow cooking time is now redundant with the ready availability of canned beans, making it an everyday staple food. If you're not a fan of red kidney beans, the nutty flavour of chickpeas makes them a good alternative. The smooth creaminess of white beans is another excellent option, creating a nutritious meal that is ideal when you want something comforting.

For **chickpea curry**, swap the cumin for black mustard seeds and use 2 × 400g (14oz) cans of chickpeas, drained and rinsed, in place of the kidney beans. After cooking, slightly crush the chickpeas with a potato masher to create a lovely textured sauce. Leave to stand for half an hour, to let the flavours infuse, or enjoy immediately.

For a **white bean curry**, swap the cumin for carom seeds (*ajwain*) and the beans for 2 × 400g (14oz) cans of white beans (try cannellini, haricot or butter beans), drained and rinsed.

I tend to always keep a few cans of chickpeas and chopped tomatoes in the cupboard, as they make for the quickest delicious meals. Here, I am playing with flavours a bit by adding a South Indian-inspired *podi* to a North Indian *chole* and the result is quite amazing. Serve with some plain rice or *pulao*, plain roti (see page 159), puri or paratha (see pages 160–70) – everything goes perfectly with this!

PODI CHOLE
Podi chickpeas

SERVES 4

2 onions, finely chopped

400g (14oz) can of chopped tomatoes

2 tablespoons Podi Masala (see page 17)

1 tablespoon Sabji Masala (see page 16)

2 × 400g (14oz) cans of chickpeas, drained and rinsed

Heat 2 tablespoons oil in a saucepan over a medium heat. Add the onions and cook for 8–10 minutes until beautifully golden.

Add the tomatoes and cook for another 10 minutes.

Add the podi masala and sabji masala along with 1 teaspoon salt and 1 teaspoon chilli powder. Mix well. Add the chickpeas along with 200ml (7fl oz) boiling water. Cover and cook for 15 minutes until thickened, then serve.

This is such a lovely dish that you can dress up or dress down, depending on what you serve it with. Keep it simple by accompanying it with rice or make it special by pairing it with some puris. It's a classic combination that is often served on special occasions, at weddings, festivals or just on a Sunday!

ALU SABJI

Potato curry

SERVES 4

1 teaspoon cumin seeds

4 tomatoes, finely chopped

1 tablespoon Sabji Masala (see page 16)

4 potatoes (Maris Piper or any other all-rounders), peeled, boiled, then cut into 2.5-cm (1-inch) pieces

1 teaspoon Chaat Masala (see page 13)

Heat 2 tablespoons oil in a saucepan and add the cumin seeds. Once they start to sizzle, add the tomatoes, cover and cook over a low heat for 10 minutes.

Add ¾ teaspoon salt and 1 teaspoon chilli powder along with the sabji masala and mix well. Add the potatoes along with 200ml (7fl oz) boiling water, cover and cook over a low heat for 10 minutes.

Finally, add the chaat masala, mix well and serve.

This is one of the dals that my mum made when we needed something light but healthy. It's nutritious but very gentle on the tummy, making it a good one for when you are a bit down or under the weather. It's great with plain rice, or enjoy with plain roti (see page 159) or just some natural yogurt.

MOONG DAL
Split mung beans

SERVES 4

300g (10½oz) split mung beans (moong dal)

1 tespoon ground turmeric

1 teaspoon cumin seeds

handful of fresh coriander, finely chopped, plus extra for serving

2 tablespoons lemon juice

Put the dal in a saucepan and add 1 litre (1¾ pints) water, 1 teaspoon salt and the ground turmeric. Bring to the boil, then reduce the heat to low and simmer for 15–20 minutes until the lentils are soft and starting to break apart.

Heat 3 tablespoons of ghee or oil of your choice in a separate small pan and add the cumin seeds. Once they start to sizzle, take the pan off the heat and add 1 teaspoon chilli powder and the chopped coriander. Mix well, then add to the dal along with the lemon juice. Mix well, sprinkle with more chopped coriander, and serve.

A stunning, light dish that is great served with plain roti (see page 159) or naan, or a plain *pulao*, such as mushroom (see page 143). If you can't get hold of paneer, you can replace it with potatoes, boiled and fried the same way.

PALAK PANEER
Spinach and Indian cheese

SERVES 4

500g (1lb 2oz) spinach leaves

4–6 garlic cloves, thinly sliced

450g (1lb) paneer, cut into 2-cm (¾-inch) cubes

2 tablespoons double cream

2 tablespoons lemon juice

Wash and drain the spinach, then put it in a saucepan along with 400ml (14fl oz) water. Cover and cook over a high heat for 5 minutes. Let it cool for a few minutes before blitzing to a purée, either in a food processor or using a hand-held stick blender.

Heat 2 tablespoons oil in a large, deep frying pan over a low heat. Add the garlic and cook for 1 minute, then add the spinach purée and cook for a further 5 minutes. Add ¾ teaspoon salt and 1 teaspoon chilli powder and mix well.

Heat enough oil for shallow-frying in a separate frying pan over a medium heat. When hot, add the paneer and cook for 1–2 minutes on each side until golden all over.

Add the fried paneer to the spinach along with the cream and lemon juice. Mix well, sprinkle with some chilli powder and serve hot.

FISH

These crunchy little fish bites serve as a perfect snack with a Tamarind Chutney (see page 180) or good old ketchup. You can turn them into a delicious starter by serving them with some Mango Salad (see page 199), too. The *podi* spices with peanuts go perfectly with the fluffy fish and crispy breadcrumbs, making these very moreish.

Crispy cod

SERVES 2

500g (1lb 2oz) cod, cut into 2.5-cm (1-inch) cubes

100g (3½oz) plain flour

1 egg

100g (3½oz) panko breadcrumbs

2 tablespoons Podi Masala (see page 17)

In a small bowl, mix ¼ teaspoon salt and ¼ teaspoon chilli powder. Sprinkle the mixture over the cod pieces and rub it in. Set aside for 10 minutes to marinate.

Prepare a bowl with the flour, a pinch of salt and a pinch of chilli powder and mix well. In a second bowl, whisk the egg with a pinch of salt and a pinch of chilli powder. In a third bowl, mix the breadcrumbs with the podi masala.

Heat enough oil for deep-frying in a deep-fat fryer or deep, heavy saucepan to 170°C (340°F), or until a cube of bread browns in 35 seconds. Dip the cod pieces first in the flour, then in the egg and finally in the breadcrumb mixture until well coated. Fry in the hot oil for 3–4 minutes until golden, turning halfway through. Remove with a slotted spoon to drain on kitchen paper and make sure the fish is cooked through. Let it sit for a minute, then sprinkle with some chilli powder and serve.

This exceptional-tasting dish is one I can eat for any meal, whether it's lunch or dinner, even on its own, but it pairs beautifully with my Carom Seed Flatbreads (see page 170) or some Herby Pulao (see page 140) or plain rice. It is really deeply delicious.

CURRY PATTA JHEENGA
Curry leaf prawns

SERVES 4

10–12 curry leaves

2 tablespoons ginger and garlic paste

2 red onions, roughly chopped

1 tablespoon Sabji Masala (see page 16)

12 raw jumbo prawns, peeled and deveined with the tails left on

Heat 3–4 tablespoons oil in a large, deep frying pan and add the curry leaves to it. Once they start to sizzle, add the ginger and garlic paste and cook for a few seconds over a low heat. Add the onions and cook over a low–medium heat for 8–10 minutes until deeply golden.

Add ½ teaspoon salt, ½ teaspoon chilli powder and the sabji masala to the pan, followed by the prawns. Cook for 3–4 minutes until the prawns are cooked through, then serve.

This is such a crowd-pleasing dish – it goes perfectly with some fluffy rice. Whether you are cooking for fussy kids, a large group or just want a healthy quick meal for yourself, this delicious cod curry will keep everyone happy. Sprinkling with some fresh coriander leaves is optional – it does not add a lot to the flavour, but it does make it look pretty on the plate.

Cod curry

SERVES 4

2 onions, finely chopped

2 tomatoes, finely chopped

1 tablespoon Sabji Masala (see page 16)

400ml (14fl oz) can of coconut milk

600g (1lb 5oz) fresh cod, cut into 5-cm (2-inch) chunks

Heat 2 tablespoons oil in a large, deep frying pan and add the onions. Cook over a low–medium heat for 6–8 minutes until lightly golden.

Add the tomatoes, cover and cook over a low heat for 10 minutes.

Add 1 teaspoon salt, 1 teaspoon chilli powder and the sabji masala to the pan and cook for 1 minute, then add the coconut milk and 200ml (7fl oz) boiling water. Cover and cook over a low heat for 10 minutes.

Add the cod chunks, cover the pan and cook for a final 5 minutes until the fish is cooked through, then serve.

MORE
WAYS
WITH

FISH CURRY

This easy fish curry is one of the quickest, healthiest, most delicious recipes you can rustle up. It's such a crowd-pleaser. I love that you can get it from storecupboard to table in a little over half an hour. In India, fish curries are often made with pomfret or rohu, but any firm, white fish will work brilliantly here. I most often make this with cod, but haddock is another great option.

For a **haddock curry**, swap the cod for 4 whole haddock fillets, each about 150g (5½oz). Keeping the fillets whole means they need a minute or two longer to cook through. They are ready when the flesh is opaque and flakes easily when tested with the tip of a knife.

The curry also lends itself to shellfish. For a **prawn curry**, replace the cod with 16 king prawns, adding them at the same time in the method and cooking for the same time. Perfect for a speedy lunch or light supper.

Living by the sea, I am lucky to get some amazing fresh fish and red sea bream is one of them. Cooking it with tandoori masala adds a little oomph to this humble dish. You can even cook it on a barbecue, if you like. Serve on the side of some Onion and Pea Rice (see page 146), or the Sour and Spicy Potatoes (see page 31) makes an amazing combination as well.

TANDOORI MACHLI

Tandoori fish

SERVES 2

1 tablespoon Tandoori Masala (see page 13)

1 whole red sea bream (roughly 600–700g/1lb 5oz–1lb 9oz), gutted and cleaned

1 lemon, cut into thin slices

handful of herbs (coriander, dill, chives, mint or parsley)

5–6 garlic cloves, thinly sliced

Preheat the oven to 200°C (400°F), Gas Mark 6.

In a small bowl, mix the tandoori masala with 2 tablespoons oil, ½ teaspoon salt and ½ teaspoon chilli powder. Make 3 cuts on both sides of the fish and rub it well with this marinade on both sides. Open the belly of the fish and stuff it with the lemon slices and most of the herbs (reserve a few herbs for serving).

Place the fish on a baking tray and roast in the oven for 20–25 minutes until cooked through. Remove from the oven and let it sit for 5 minutes.

Heat 2 tablespoons oil in a small pan and add the garlic, cook for 2 minutes, then remove from the heat and add a pinch of chilli powder and a few sprigs of the reserved herbs. Pour the mixture over the cooked fish and serve.

Piping hot prawn curry piled on top of plain fluffy basmati rice is simply heaven. Light, fresh and delicious is the only way to describe this stunning dish.

JHEENGA CURRY

Prawn curry

SERVES 4

2 tablespoons ginger and garlic paste

70g (2½oz) tomato purée

1 tablespoon Sabji Masala (see page 16)

400ml (14fl oz) can of coconut milk

12–16 raw jumbo prawns, peeled and deveined (you can leave the heads and tails on or remove them, as you prefer)

Heat 2 tablespoons oil in a large, deep frying pan, add the ginger and garlic paste and cook over a low heat for 1 minute. Add the tomato purée along with 100ml (3½fl oz) water, bring to the boil, then cover and cook over a low heat for 10–15 minutes.

Add ½ teaspoon salt, 1 teaspoon chilli powder and the sabji masala to the pan, followed by the coconut milk and another 100ml (3½fl oz) water. Bring to the boil, then cook over a low heat for a further 10 minutes or until the sauce has thickened.

Add the prawns and cook for a final 5 minutes over a medium heat until cooked through, then serve.

This is something I make specially for me, as my family are not big on crab yet (maybe one day!). I love using crab in a curry, as the spices work perfectly with the intense flavour of the meat. The addition of spinach is another thing I like, as it adds a bit more bite and colour to the dish. This goes beautifully with some plain white rice.

Crab curry

SERVES 2

2 onions, finely chopped

1 teaspoon Sabji Masala (see page 16)

1 teaspoon Garam Masala (see page 16)

100g (3½oz) spinach, finely chopped

200g (7oz) white crab meat

Heat 2 tablespoons oil in a large, deep frying pan, add the onions and cook over a low heat for about 8 minutes until golden.

Add the sabji masala and garam masala along with ½ teaspoon salt and ½ teaspoon chilli powder, then add 200ml (7fl oz) boiling water along with the spinach and crab meat. Cook for 4–5 minutes until everything is bubbling hot, then serve.

Great for a snack with some Coriander Chutney (see page 184) or with a side of some Mango Salad (see page 199), you could also serve this for dinner with an Onion and Pea or Herby Pulao (see pages 146 or 140).

MACHLI FRY

Fish fry

SERVES 2

150g (5½oz) gram flour (besan)

1 tablespoon ginger and garlic paste

1 tablespoon lemon juice

600g (1lb 5oz) whole sea bass, gutted and cleaned, cut into 1-cm (½-inch) slices

½ teaspoon Chaat Masala (see page 13)

Start by making the batter for the fish. In a bowl, combine the gram flour with the ginger and garlic paste, lemon juice, ½ teaspoon salt, ½ teaspoon chilli powder and 120ml (4fl oz) water. Mix well.

Heat enough oil for deep-frying in a deep-fat fryer or deep, heavy saucepan to 160°C (320°F), or until a cube of bread browns in 40 seconds. Dip the fish pieces in the batter and fry for 5–6 minutes in total, turning over halfway through. Remove with a slotted spoon to drain on kitchen paper and make sure the fish is cooked through and crispy.

Sprinkle the chaat masala on top and serve.

CHICKEN

This is a winning chicken recipe. The black pepper adds to the warmth and depth of flavour of this simple, healthy, nutritious meal. This would be great with any sides, whether you go for a simple roti (see page 159), paratha (see pages 160–70) or even a *pulao* of your choice, it matches everything perfectly.

KALI MIRCH MURGH
Pepper chicken

SERVES 4

2 onions, thinly sliced

1 tablespoon ginger and garlic paste

1 tablespoon black peppercorns

1 teaspoon Garam Masala (see page 16)

8 skinless, bone-in chicken thighs

Heat 2 tablespoons oil in a large, deep frying pan. Add the onions and cook over a low–medium heat for 10 minutes until deeply golden. Add the ginger and garlic paste and cook for another minute.

Meanwhile, dry-roast the peppercorns in a separate frying pan for 2–3 minutes until fragrant. Crush them in a pestle and mortar to a fine powder.

Add 1 teaspoon salt, 1 teaspoon chilli powder and the garam masala to the onion pan, then add the chicken thighs along with 200ml (7fl oz) water and mix it all well. Cover and cook over a low heat for 20 minutes.

Uncover the pan, add the ground pepper, then cover again and cook for another 20 minutes until the chicken is cooked through. Serve.

These are my absolute favourite little chicken bites to eat with some Coriander Chutney (see page 184). They make a perfect starter or snack, enjoyed hot on their own, or they also serve as a great side with some paratha (see pages 160–70), plain roti (see page 159) or even a simple *pulao*.

MURG TIKKA

Chicken tikka

SERVES 4

60g (2¼oz) gram flour (besan)

150g (5½oz) Greek yogurt

50g (1¾oz) Cheddar cheese, grated

8 skinless, boneless chicken thighs, cut into 2.5–5-cm (1–2-inch) chunks

1 teaspoon Chaat Masala (see page 13)

Dry-roast the gram flour in a frying pan for 2–3 minutes over a low heat until lightly golden and fragrant. Transfer it to a bowl with the yogurt and cheese and add 1 teaspoon salt and 1 teaspoon chilli powder. Mix well. Add the chicken pieces and turn until thoroughly coated.

Heat a little oil for shallow-frying in a large, deep frying pan and cook the chicken in batches over a medium heat for 8–10 minutes, turning frequently until golden and cooked through. Alternatively, thread the chicken pieces onto skewers and cook on a barbecue.

Once cooked, sprinkle with the chaat masala and serve.

I have many variations of this simple yogurt chicken curry. You can make it with boneless chicken pieces, but if you have time cook it with chicken on the bone for added depth of flavour. Serve with some warm roti (see page 159) or plain rice.

DAHI MURG
Yogurt chicken

SERVES 4

250g (9oz) natural yogurt

2 tablespoons Tandoori Masala (see page 13)

8 skinless, boneless chicken thighs, each cut into 4 pieces

4 onions, roughly chopped

2 tablespoons ginger and garlic paste

Put the yogurt in a bowl with 1 teaspoon salt, 1 teaspoon chilli powder and the tandoori masala and mix well. Add the chicken pieces and turn to coat them well. Cover and leave to marinate for 1 hour or overnight in the refrigerator.

Heat 2–3 tablespoons ghee or oil in a large, deep frying pan, then add the onions. Cook over a medium heat for 8–10 minutes until deeply golden. Add the ginger and garlic paste and cook for another minute, then add the marinated chicken along with its marinade and mix well. Cover and cook over a low heat for 15 minutes.

Uncover the pan and continue to cook over a high heat for 10 minutes. Turn off the heat and let it sit for a final 10 minutes before serving.

This very light and fresh chicken dish is easily made with the regular curry powder that is available in all supermarkets – you don't have to go to a specialist store for it. Perfectly paired with coconut milk, this is great with just some plain rice.

NARIYAL MURG

Coconut chicken curry

SERVES 4

2 onions, finely chopped

2.5-cm (1-inch) piece of fresh root ginger, peeled and finely chopped

8 skinless, bone-in chicken thighs

2 tablespoons curry powder

400ml (14fl oz) can of coconut milk

Heat 3 tablespoons oil in a large, deep frying pan and add the onions. Cook over a medium heat for 6–8 minutes until golden, then add the ginger and cook for 2 minutes.

Add the chicken and cook over a high heat for 5 minutes.

Add 1 teaspoon salt and 1 teaspoon chilli powder along with the curry powder and cook for 2 minutes, then add the coconut milk and 100ml (3½fl oz) boiling water. Cover and cook for 40 minutes over a low–medium heat until the chicken is cooked through, then serve.

This is one of my favourite ways to enjoy roast chicken – the marinade with fragrant and lively tandoori masala takes the flavours of the chicken to the next level. You can use a whole chicken or even chicken legs or thighs for smaller portions – you just need to adjust the cooking time. Enjoy with some salad in the summer or roast potatoes or *pulao* in winter.

TANDOORI MURG

Tandoori roast chicken

SERVES 4

2 tablespoons ginger and garlic paste

150g (5½oz) Greek yogurt

2 tablespoons Tandoori Masala (see page 13)

2 tablespoons tomato purée

1 × 1.5kg (3lb 5oz) chicken, spatchcocked

In a medium bowl, combine the ginger and garlic paste with the yogurt, tandoori masala, tomato purée, 1 teaspoon salt, 1 teaspoon chilli powder and 2 tablespoons oil. Mix well.

Place the chicken in a roasting tin and rub the marinade all over it. Cover and leave to marinate for 1 hour, or overnight in the refrigerator, if possible.

Preheat the oven to 200°C (400°F), Gas Mark 6.

Roast the chicken for 1 hour, or until cooked through. Remove from the oven and let it rest for 5 minutes before serving.

This is an interesting one, as it uses fresh fenugreek leaves, which you can find in Asian supermarkets. In case you can't get to one, you can use 3 tablespoons dried fenugreek leaves (*kasuri methi*) instead, which is available in all supermarkets. Either way, this is one to try with some plain roti (see page 159) or paratha (see pages 160–70).

METHI MURG

Fenugreek chicken

SERVES 4

1 bunch of fresh fenugreek leaves

2 onions, thinly sliced

2 tablespoons ginger and garlic paste

10 skinless, boneless chicken thighs, cut into 5-cm (2-inch) chunks

1 tablespoon Garam Masala (see page 16)

Start by prepping the fenugreek. Break the leaves off the stems, wash, then roughly chop.

Heat 2 tablespoons oil in a large, deep frying pan and add the onions. Cook over a medium heat for 6–8 minutes until golden. Add the ginger and garlic paste and cook for another 2 minutes.

Add the chicken and cook over a high heat for 5 minutes.

Add the garam masala along with 1 teaspoon salt and 1 teaspoon chilli powder, then add the fenugreek leaves, cover and cook over a low–medium heat for 5 minutes.

Uncover the pan and cook for a final 2 minutes over a high heat, then serve.

MORE
WAYS
WITH

CHICKEN

North Indian *Methi Murg* is a beautifully flavourful dish.
The bitter freshness of fenugreek leaves is an ideal combination
with tender chicken. Fenugreek can be a difficult ingredient to
source, however, so it's good to know there are some easy variations
that also work well. Spinach and tomatoes are readily available and
bring a gentle bitter tang and plenty of nourishment to enrich the
dish. And potatoes make a very simple addition – ideal when you
need something comforting and filling, fast.

For **spinach chicken**, swap the onions for 2 thinly sliced tomatoes,
cooking them in the oil first. Replace the fenugreek with 200g (7oz)
spinach leaves, roughly chopped.

For **potato chicken**, swap the fenugreek for 2 potatoes, cut into
2.5-cm (1-inch) cubes. Add the potatoes to the pan before you
add the chicken, cooking the pieces for 5 minutes to take on
a little colour. When you add the spices, 2 tablespoons of
additional water will help the potatoes to steam and soften
until cooked through.

Piping hot *podi* chicken served on a simple *pulao* or with some paratha (see pages 160–70) is comforting and oh so delicious. You can choose to serve with plain rice or plain roti (see page 159) instead, but the sides don't really matter with this very wholesome chicken curry.

PODI MURG
Podi chicken

SERVES 4

20 curry leaves

2 onions, finely chopped

8 skinless, bone-in chicken thighs

1 tablespoon Sabji Masala (see page 16)

1 tablespoon Podi Masala (see page 17)

Heat 2 tablespoons oil in a large, deep frying pan over a low heat and add the curry leaves. Cook for a few seconds, then add the onions and cook for 10 minutes until deeply golden.

Add the chicken and cook over a high heat for 5 minutes, turning from time to time, to get a bit of colour on it.

Add 1 teaspoon salt and 1 teaspoon chilli powder along with the sabji masala, then add 500ml (18fl oz) water. Bring to the boil, then cover and cook over a low–medium heat for 30 minutes.

Uncover the pan, add the podi masala and mix well. Cook for a final 5–10 minutes over a high heat until the curry has thickened and the chicken is cooked through, then serve.

Over the years, I have encountered so many variations of egg curry, which is a popular dish in India. When I first started writing about Indian food, people would often look at me with doubt when I mentioned curry made with eggs and I had to tell them just how delicious and healthy the dish is. Served with paratha (see pages 160–70), naan or just some plain roti (see page 159), I'm certain you will enjoy it.

ANDA CURRY

Egg curry

SERVES 4

8 eggs

2 tablespoons ginger and garlic paste

400g (14oz) can of chopped tomatoes

1 teaspoon Garam Masala (see page 16)

3 tablespoons natural yogurt

Put the eggs in a saucepan of boiling water and boil for 8 minutes. Drain and set aside for a minute before peeling and cutting the eggs in half.

Heat enough oil for shallow frying in a frying pan and cook the eggs over a high heat for 1–2 minutes on each side until golden. Set aside.

Heat 2 tablespoons oil in a large, deep frying pan over a low heat. Add the ginger and garlic paste and cook for 2 minutes, then add the tomatoes along with 200ml (7fl oz) water and bring to the boil. Cover and cook over a low–medium heat for 20 minutes.

Add 1 teaspoon salt, 1 teaspoon chilli powder, ½ teaspoon black pepper and 1 teaspoon sugar to the pan along with the garam masala and mix it all well, then add the yogurt and eggs and cook for a final 5 minutes over a low heat.

Serve hot.

RICE

This is a must-try rice dish. Being a fan of cauliflower, this recipe is really special to me. The combination of the cauliflower along with the podi masala with peanuts in it is just so delicious. It's also a great way to jazz up leftover rice. Serve on its own or with some Coconut Chutney (see page 181) for added flavour.

PODI GOBHI CHAWAL
Podi cauliflower rice

SERVES 4

200g (7oz) basmati rice (or use 600g/1lb 5oz pre-cooked/leftover rice)

10–12 fresh curry leaves

1 small cauliflower, cut into small florets

3 tablespoons Podi Masala (see page 17)

1 teaspoon ground turmeric

Cook the rice according to the instructions on the packet (unless you are using pre-cooked rice).

Heat 2 tablespoons oil in a saucepan and add the curry leaves followed by the cauliflower florets. Add 2 tablespoons water, cover and cook over a medium heat for 10 minutes.

Add the podi masala and turmeric to the pan along with 1 teaspoon salt and 1 teaspoon chilli powder. Mix well, then add the cooked rice and mix again. Cook over a high heat for a final 2 minutes, then serve.

MORE
WAYS
WITH

PODI RICE

This nutty-flavoured rice dish hails from South India.
I love the punchy spice mix blended with the milder flavour
of the cauliflower – it makes a fantastic combination. If cauliflower
isn't your thing, it's a very versatile recipe. Potatoes and green beans
make ideal substitutions and you can freshen it up with chopped
herbs too, if you prefer.

For **podi potato rice**, replace the cauliflower with 2 potatoes,
cut into 2.5-cm (1-inch) cubes, cooking them in the same way.
Omit the turmeric and instead add a handful of finely chopped
fresh coriander at the same time as the cooked rice goes in.

To make **podi beans rice**, add a teaspoon of black mustard seeds
to the pan and let them sizzle a little before the curry leaves go in.
Swap the cauliflower for 250g (9oz) fine green beans, each halved.
They will need less cooking time, 2–3 minutes should be enough.
You can omit the turmeric.

This is a really fresh *pulao* if ever there was one. Herby, vibrant and aromatic, it's great with absolutely any curry, dal or *sabji*. It's also good with just a raita (see pages 185–93) and some Masala Papad (see page 28) on the side. You can play around with the herbs to suit your preference – replace the coriander with parsley or the dill with chives, it's your choice.

Herby pulao

SERVES 4

1½ teaspoons cumin seeds

10–12 fresh curry leaves

300g (10½oz) basmati rice

1 tablespoon Garam Masala (see page 16)

20g (¾oz) mixed herbs (coriander, mint and dill), plus extra for serving

Heat 2 tablespoons oil in a saucepan, add the cumin seeds and let them sizzle, then add the curry leaves. Add the rice along with the garam masala, 1 teaspoon salt and 1 teaspoon chilli powder. Add the herbs and then 600ml (20fl oz) boiling water to the pan. Cover and cook over a low heat for 15 minutes.

Remove from the heat and let it sit with the lid on for another 10 minutes. Scatter with some mixed herbs before serving.

This is a delicious, healthy rice dish that is ready in no time. I am using chestnut mushrooms, but you can use any other mushroom of your choice. Serve with a cooling raita (see pages 185–93).

Mushroom rice

SERVES 4

1 onion, thinly sliced

4–5 garlic cloves, finely chopped

400–500g (14oz–1lb 2oz) chestnut mushrooms, thinly sliced

1 teaspoon ground cumin

300g (10½oz) basmati rice

Heat 2 tablespoons oil in a saucepan, add the onions and cook over a medium heat for 5 minutes until softened. Add the garlic and cook for 2 minutes.

Add the mushrooms and cook over a medium heat for 10 minutes until softened and the water is cooked out.

Add 1 teaspoon salt, 1 teaspoon chilli powder, the ground cumin and the rice. Mix well, then add 600ml (20fl oz) boiling water. Cover and cook for 15 minutes.

Remove from the heat and let it sit with the lid on for another 10 minutes before serving.

A lively bright rice to accompany some raita (see pages 185–93) or a chicken curry. You can add a couple of extra ingredients, if you like, such as some dried red chillies and curry leaves when you add the peanuts, but it will taste amazing even if you just make the recipe as it is.

NIMBU CHAWAL

Lemon rice

SERVES 4

60g (2¼oz) peanuts, skin on

1 teaspoon black mustard seeds

1 tablespoon Sabji Masala (see page 16)

300g (10½oz) basmati rice

2 tablespoons lemon juice

Crush the peanuts in a pestle and mortar until the nuts have broken up, but don't let them turn to powder.

Heat 2 tablespoons oil in a saucepan and add the mustard seeds, then add the crushed peanuts to the pan and cook over a low heat for 2 minutes until they change colour and get nice and toasted.

Add 1 teaspoon salt and 1 teaspoon chilli powder along with the sabji masala, then add the rice along with 600ml (20fl oz) boiling water. Cover and cook for 10 minutes, then add the lemon juice, mix well, re-cover and cook for another 5 minutes.

Remove from the heat and let it sit with the lid on for 10 minutes before serving.

This is one of those meals I cook when I want something quick, easy and comforting. This onion and pea *pulao* is heavenly with just some Boondi Raita (see page 191). It's a meal I often cook when we get back home after being out all day or from travelling. It's also a great dish to make to accompany any curry, dal or *sabji* you might be cooking. Being vegan, healthy and gluten-free, it ticks a lot of boxes when cooking for a crowd, too.

MATAR PULAO
Onion and pea rice

SERVES 4

1 teaspoon cumin seeds
2 onions, thinly sliced
150g (5½oz) frozen peas
1½ teaspoons ground cumin
300g (10½oz) basmati rice

Heat 2 tablespoons of oil in a saucepan and add the cumin seeds. Once they start to sizzle, add the onions and cook over a medium heat for 5–6 minutes until lightly golden.

Add the peas along with 1 teaspoon salt, 1 teaspoon chilli powder and the ground cumin. Give it a good mix, then add the rice and 600ml (20fl oz) boiling water. Let it bubble, put a lid on and cook over a low heat for 15 minutes.

Remove from the heat and let it sit with the lid on for another 10 minutes before sprinkling with chilli powder and serving.

This is one dish that never fails to deliver. I always have cans of chickpeas in the cupboard because they are a shortcut to making the quickest healthy meal. Whether you add them to a curry or salad or this fluffy happy rice dish, it's a speedy way to add some nutrition to a meal. This is one of my daughter's favourite things for her lunchbox. At home, you can serve this with a chutney (see pages 180–4) or some raita (see pages 185–93).

CHOLE CHAWAL
Chickpea rice

SERVES 4

2 teaspoons cumin seeds

2 onions, roughly chopped

1 tablespoon Sabji Masala (see page 16)

400g (14oz) can of chickpeas, drained and rinsed

300g (10½oz) basmati rice, cooked

Heat 2 tablespoons oil in a saucepan and add the cumin seeds. Once they start to sizzle, add the onions and cook over a medium heat for 6–8 minutes until golden.

Add 1 teaspoon salt and 1 teaspoon chilli powder along with the sabji masala to the pan, then add the chickpeas and cook for 2 minutes over a high heat.

Add the cooked rice, mix well and cook for a final 5 minutes over a low heat before serving.

If you are fond of prawns, then this *pulao* is the perfect meal for you. The nutty podi masala with the onions and curry leaves is all you need to make the prawns taste amazing. Serve this on its own or with some Coconut Chutney (see page 181), if you like.

JHEENGA PULAO
Prawn rice

SERVES 4

15–20 curry leaves

3 onions, thinly sliced

2 tablespoons Podi Masala (see page 17)

12 raw jumbo prawns, peeled and deveined with the tails left on

300g (10½oz) basmati rice

Heat 2 tablespoons oil in a large, deep frying pan and add the curry leaves. Once they start to sizzle, add the onions and cook over a low heat for 5–6 minutes until beginning to colour.

Add the podi masala, 1 teaspoon salt, 1 teaspoon chilli powder and the prawns and stir to combine. Next, add the rice along with 600ml (20fl oz) boiling water. Mix it all well, cover and cook for 15 minutes.

Remove from the heat and let it sit with the lid on for another 10 minutes before serving.

A warming *pulao* with the perfect spicing to keep it simple and super-quick to make. You can enjoy this piping hot with a raita (see pages 185–93) on the side to cool it down or just natural yogurt will work well, too. You can even try this with chicken thighs on the bone for extra flavour – just cook the thighs for 30 minutes with the onions before adding the rice to the pan.

MURG PULAO
Chicken rice

SERVES 4

1½ teaspoons cumin seeds

2 onions, thinly sliced

8 skinless, boneless chicken thighs, cut into 2.5-cm (1-inch) chunks

1 tablespoon Tandoori Masala (see page 13)

300g (10½oz) basmati rice

Heat 2 tablespoons oil in a large, deep frying pan and add the cumin seeds. Once they start to sizzle, add the onions and cook over a low–medium heat for 6–8 minutes until golden.

Add the chicken to the pan along with 1 teaspoon salt, 1 teaspoon chilli powder and the tandoori masala. Cook over a high heat for 5 minutes.

Add the rice along with 600ml (20fl oz) boiling water. Cover and cook over a low heat for 15 minutes.

Remove from the heat and let it sit with the lid on for another 10 minutes, then open the lid and fluff up with a fork before serving.

BREADS

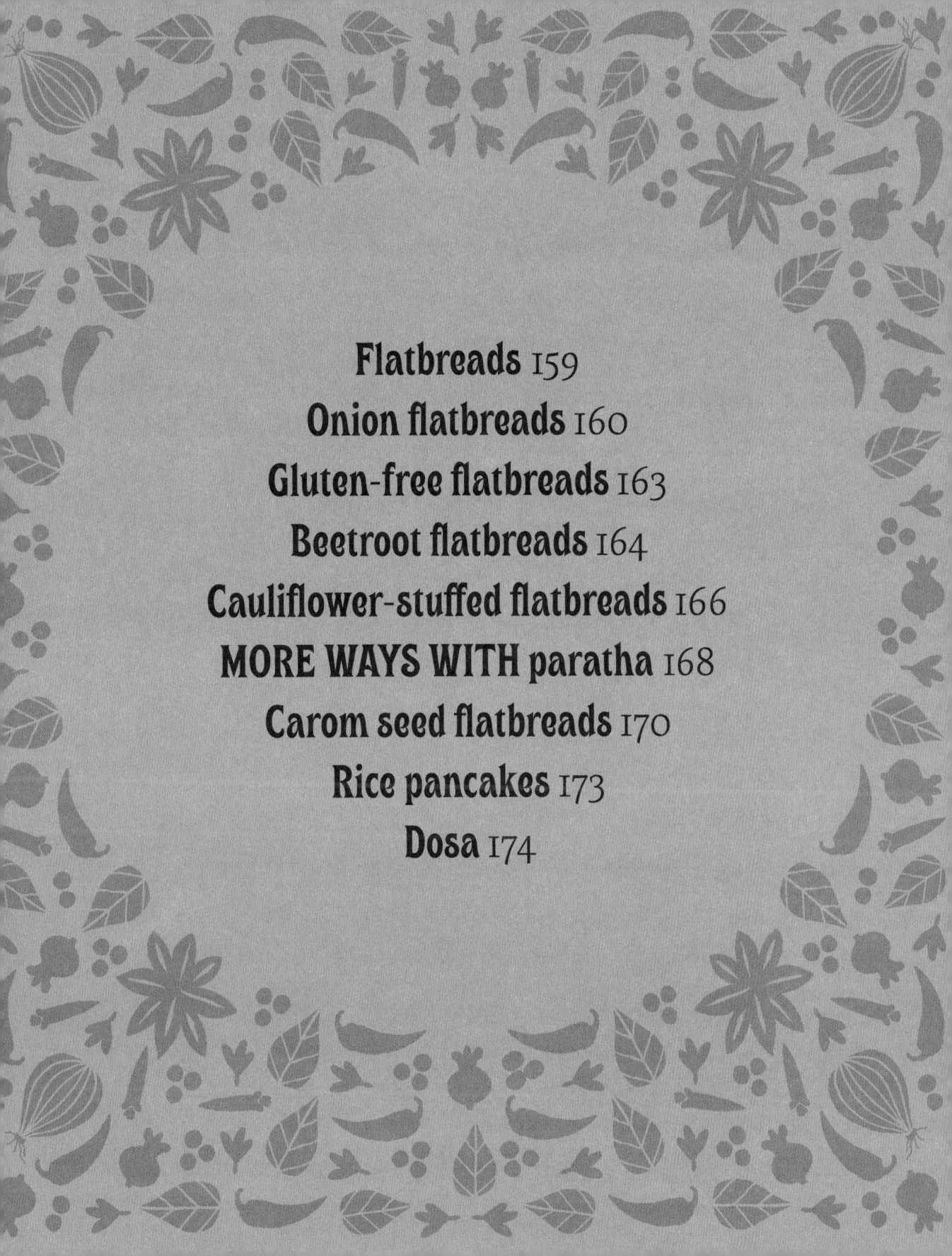

A staple in every Indian kitchen – in India or anywhere else in the world – you will see these called *roti* or *chapatti* or *phulka* – all names that mean the same thing. This is one thing that's so tricky to find in a restaurant, where you can get some of the best naans or paratha, but roti are something that always tastes best when made at home. And, you really do only need two things to create this delicious, healthy, amazing flatbread – flour and water!

ROTI
Flatbreads

MAKES 12

300g (10½oz) chapatti flour (atta), plus extra for dusting

Put the flour in a bowl and slowly add 200–220ml (7–8fl oz) water – not all at once. You want to add a little and mix before adding more. Once you have a nice soft dough, knead for a minute, then cover and let it rest for at least 15–20 minutes. This resting is key to getting nice soft rotis.

Divide the rested dough into 12 portions. Use a rolling pin to roll out each portion on a floured work surface into a thin disc, 15–18cm (6–7 inches) in diameter.

Heat a frying pan until hot. Cook each roti on one side for a few seconds. Once you can spot a few bubbles forming, turn it over. After a few seconds, turn it back over and press gently with a spatula – this will help it to puff up and is a technique you will master with practise. Once cooked, brush with some ghee and serve.

These are best enjoyed when freshly made, but if you are making them a few hours in advance, make sure to wrap the cooked roti in a clean cloth or some kitchen foil and store in an airtight container to keep them nice and soft. Alternatively, you can keep the dough in an airtight container in the refrigerator and use it for up to 4 days.

Crispy on the edges with crunchy onion bits inside, these paratha are so delicious and great with just some butter on top or a chutney on the side (see pages 180–4). They are also great with any curry, dal or *sabji*.

PYAAZ KA PARATHA
Onion flatbreads

MAKES 8

300g (10½oz) chapatti flour (atta), plus extra for dusting

½ teaspoon ground turmeric

2 onions, finely chopped

handful of fresh coriander, finely chopped

1 teaspoon Tandoori Masala (see page 13)

In a large bowl, combine the flour with the turmeric, ½ teaspoon salt and ½ teaspoon chilli powder. Mix well. Slowly add around 230ml (8fl oz) water and bring it together into a soft dough. Knead for a few seconds, then cover and let it rest for 10–15 minutes.

In a bowl, combine the onions, coriander and tandoori masala with ½ teaspoon salt and mix well.

Divide the rested dough into 8 portions. Use a rolling pin to roll out each portion into a thin disc, about 10cm (4 inches) in diameter. Sprinkle an eighth of the onion mixture over the dough and press it in slightly. Roll each disc into a sausage and then twist into a coil. Dust with a bit of flour, then roll each portion out into a circle again.

Heat a frying pan until hot, then cook each paratha for 1 minute on each side before adding 1 teaspoon oil to the pan and cooking until golden and crispy on both sides, turning as needed.

Repeat until all the paratha are cooked, then serve.

These amazing gluten-free paratha taste incredible. Buckwheat flour is used a lot for flatbreads in India and makes for perfect paratha. Enjoy them nice and hot – they are a meal on their own with so much flavour and great texture. Serve with some butter, if you want, or a pickle, chutney (see pages 180–4) or raita (see pages 185–93).

KUTTU PARATHA
Gluten-free flatbreads

MAKES 8

200g (7oz) buckwheat flour, plus extra for dusting

2 potatoes, peeled, boiled, then grated

handful of fresh coriander, finely chopped

1 green chilli, finely chopped

1 teaspoon Garam Masala (see page 16)

In a large bowl, mix together the flour, grated potato, coriander, green chilli and garam masala with ½ teaspoon salt and ½ teaspoon chilli powder. Slowly add 100ml (3½fl oz) water (you might not need all of it) and bring it together to a soft dough. Cover and let it rest for 10 minutes.

Divide the rested dough into 8 portions. Use a rolling pin to roll each portion into a 7.5-cm (3-inch) circle. Brush each disc with ½ teaspoon oil or ghee, fold the dough half and then in half again, and gently form into a triangle shape. Sprinkle some flour on the surface and roll each one out again to a roughly 15-cm (6-inch) triangle.

Heat a frying pan until hot. Cook each paratha for 1 minute on each side, then add ½ teaspoon oil or ghee to each side and cook until golden and crispy, turning as needed.

Repeat until all the paratha are cooked, then serve.

These breads are one of my favourite ways to eat beetroot – they are so nutritious and easy to make, and the cumin brings warmth to the earthy beetroot. They are great to enjoy on their own or with some raita (see pages 185–93), chutney (see pages 180–4) or any curry or *sabji*. They also work so well as a wrap for your lunch or a picnic.

CHUKUNDER PARATHA
Beetroot flatbreads

MAKES 10

1 teaspoon cumin seeds

2.5-cm (1-inch) piece of fresh root ginger, peeled and roughly chopped

3 beetroots (about 400g/ 14oz in total), peeled and chopped into small chunks

300g (10½oz) chapatti flour (atta), plus extra or dusting

1 teaspoon ground cumin

Heat 2 tablespoons oil in a pan and add the cumin seeds. Once they start to sizzle, add the ginger and cook for a minute. Add the beetroot to the pan along with 100ml (3½fl oz) water. Cover and cook over a low–medium heat for 15 minutes.

Remove from the heat and leave to cool. Once cooled, blitz to a purée in a food processor. Transfer to a bowl.

Add the flour and ground cumin to the purée along with ½ teaspoon salt and ½ teaspoon chilli powder. Knead to a soft dough. You might need to add 1 or 2 tablespoons water to help bring it together. Cover and let it rest for 15 minutes.

Divide the rested dough into 10 portions. Use a rolling pin to roll out each portion into a thin disc, about 5–7.5cm (2–3 inches) in diameter. Brush with some ghee or oil, roll each disc into a sausage and then twist into a coil. Dust with a bit of flour, then roll each portion out into a circle again.

Heat a frying pan until hot, then cook each paratha for 1 minute on each side before adding 1 teaspoon oil to the pan and cooking until golden and crispy on both sides, turning as needed.

Repeat until all the paratha are cooked, then serve.

This is one of my favourite paratha – the flavour of cauliflower cooked with the aromatic carom seeds is just perfect, especially when served with any raita (see pages 185–93) or just some yogurt. They are great to make in advance and just cook with a little oil when ready to eat. They're perfect for packed lunches and picnics, too.

GOBHI PARATHA
Cauliflower-stuffed flatbreads

MAKES 10

400g (14oz) cauliflower, grated

1 teaspoon carom seeds (ajwain)

1 teaspoon Garam Masala (see page 16)

1 tablespoon grated fresh root ginger

300g (10½oz) chapatti flour (atta), plus extra for dusting

Put the cauliflower in a bowl along with the carom seeds, garam masala, ginger, 1 teaspoon salt and 1 teaspoon chilli powder. Mix it all well.

In a separate large bowl, mix the chapatti flour with ½ teaspoon salt and slowly add 220ml (8fl oz) water. Add little at a time and mix before adding any more. Knead for a minute until you have a nice soft dough, then cover and let it rest for 15–20 minutes.

Divide the rested dough into 10 portions. Use a rolling pin to roll out each portion into a thin disc, about 7.5–10cm (3–4 inches) in diameter. Put a tenth of the cauliflower filling mixture in the middle of the circle, then pinch the dough in on all sides to seal it inside. Dust with a bit of flour, then roll each portion out into a 15-cm (6-inch) circle.

Heat a frying pan until hot. Cook each paratha for a couple of minutes on each side over a medium heat, then add 1 teaspoon ghee or oil to each side and cook until golden and crispy, turning as needed.

Repeat until all the paratha are cooked, then serve nice and hot.

MORE
WAYS
WITH

PARATHA

Stuffed paratha are hugely adaptable and many ingredients lend themselves to filling these delicious flatbreads. They are a great way to get more vegetables into your diet, too. Cauliflower and carom seeds are one of my all-time favourite combos, but you can play around with other mashable and grateable vegetables or chopped herbs and different spice combinations until you find your own favourite. I've given you paneer and potato fillings here, but you could also try chopped spinach, fresh coriander or mashed peas. In the Punjab, they make a lovely version with grated mooli (daikon radish) and finely chopped green chillies.

For **paneer paratha**, swap the cauliflower for 450g (1lb) grated paneer and the carom seeds for the same amount of mustard seeds. The basic method remains identical.

For **potato paratha**, use 4 boiled and mashed potatoes in place of the cauliflower and swap the ginger for 4 crushed cloves of garlic. These are delicious eaten for breakfast with some yogurt and chutney.

These used to be my favourite paratha when I was growing up. My mum would often make them for our lunchboxes and spread some mango pickle in the paratha before rolling it up. These are so delicious piping hot, but are also great at room temperature. Enjoy with just pickle or some curry or *sabji* of your choice. And remember to make a few extra for your lunch!

NAMAK AJWAIN PARATHA

Carom seed flatbreads

MAKES 12

400g (14oz) chapatti flour (atta), plus extra for dusting

1 teaspoon carom seeds (ajwain)

In a large bowl, combine the flour with 1 teaspoon salt, 1 teaspoon chilli powder and the carom seeds. Give it a mix, then add 2 tablespoons ghee or oil of your choice. Slowly add about 300ml (½ pint) water to the mixture (you might not need all the water, or may need a bit more). Knead for a few seconds until you have a soft dough. Cover and let it rest for at least 15 minutes.

Divide the rested dough into 12 portions. Use a rolling pin to roll each portion into a 7.5-cm (3-inch) circle. Brush each disc with ½ teaspoon oil or ghee, fold the dough half and then in half again, and gently form into a triangle shape. Sprinkle some flour on the surface and roll each one out again to a roughly 15-cm (6-inch) triangle.

Heat a frying pan until hot. Cook each paratha for 1 minute on each side, then add 1 teaspoon oil or ghee to the pan and cook for another minute until golden and crispy, turning as needed.

Repeat until all the paratha are cooked. Serve hot with some pickle or raita.

You can prepare this dough ahead and store it in an airtight container in the refrigerator for up to 4 days, to make fresh paratha whenever you want.

A popular South Indian dish, *uttapam* is served with either *sambhar* (a lentil and vegetable stew) or just some Coconut Chutney (see page 181). Once you have tried it with the classic topping of onion and tomato, then you can try other toppings of your choice – some grated paneer or cheese, garlic, green chillies … just go for your favourites.

UTTAPAM
Rice pancakes

SERVES 4

200g (7oz) white basmati rice

35g (1¼oz) urid dal (split skinless black lentils)

2 onions, finely chopped

2 tomatoes, finely chopped

handful of fresh coriander, finely chopped, plus extra for serving

Soak the rice and dal in plenty of water overnight, in separate containers.

The next day, drain, then blend the soaked rice and dal separately in a blender along with 50–100ml (2–3½fl oz) water until they are both as smooth as a purée. Once blended, combine them in a bowl, cover and leave in a warm part of the kitchen to ferment for 24 hours. The batter will rise a little and smell sour. Transfer it to the refrigerator until you are ready to cook.

When ready to cook, combine the onions, tomatoes and coriander in a bowl with ½ teaspoon salt and ½ teaspoon chilli powder. Set aside.

Check the batter is the right consistency: it should be easy to spread, like a thick crêpe batter, so add enough water accordingly.

Heat a frying pan and add a few drops of oil. Once hot, wipe it carefully with kitchen paper so it is greased but dry. Pour a ladleful of batter into the pan and use the bottom of the ladle to spread it slightly. Sprinkle some of the onion mixture on top. Drizzle 1 teaspoon of oil around the edge of the pancake and cook for a couple of minutes on each side until it turns golden. Repeat until you have used up all the batter. Sprinkle with chopped coriander, then serve.

A staple in South Indian kitchens, this bread is a favourite of many Indians around the world. This plain dosa is delicious with classic sides of chutney (see pages 180–4) and *sambhar*, or you can enjoy it with different curries and dal too. Alternatively, just fill it with some Sour and Spicy Potatoes (see page 31).

Dosa

MAKES 20

300g (10½oz) basmati rice
100g (3½oz) urid dal (split skinless black lentils)
10g (¼oz) fenugreek seeds

Soak the rice overnight in 500ml (18fl oz) water. At the same time, in a separate bowl, soak the urid dal and fenugreek seeds together in 400ml (14fl oz) water.

The next day, drain then blend the soaked rice and dal separately. Add a little extra water if you have to, but be careful, as you want them to be thick pastes. Once blended, combine them in a bowl, cover and leave in a warm part of the kitchen to ferment for 24 hours. The batter will rise a little and smell sour. Transfer it to the refrigerator until you are ready to cook.

Check the batter is the right consistency: it should be easy to spread, like crêpe batter, so add water accordingly.

Heat a frying pan and add a few drops of oil. Once it is hot, wipe it carefully with kitchen paper so that the pan is greased but dry. Pour a ladleful of batter into the pan and use the bottom of the ladle to spread it over the base, making a large, thin dosa. Drizzle 1 teaspoon oil around the edge of the dosa and cook until the dosa turns golden. Fold it in half and remove from the pan. Repeat with the remaining batter.

CHUTNEYS
& MORE

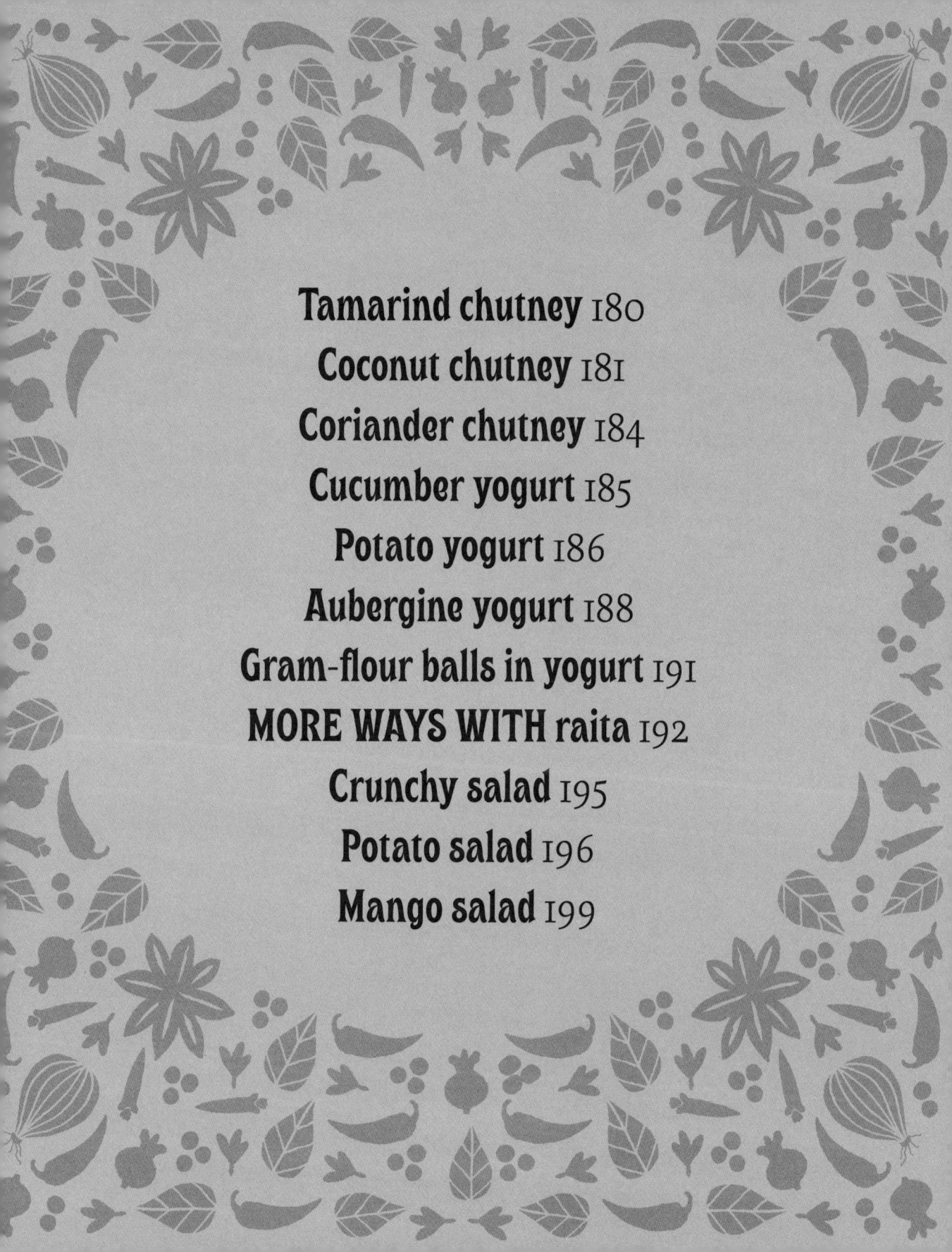

This is one of the key chutneys you need to make Indian *chaat*. A perfect balance of sweet, sour and spicy, it's a great chutney to always have in the refrigerator. You must use the tamarind pulp that comes with the seeds. You can buy it and jaggery in Asian supermarkets. Once cooled, you can store it in a jar in the refrigerator for a good 3–4 months. It might thicken once cooled, but you can add a splash of water when you want to use it.

IMLI CHUTNEY

Tamarind chutney

75g (2¾oz) tamarind pulp
50g (1¾oz) jaggery
50g (1¾oz) dates, pitted
¼ teaspoon ground cumin
¼ teaspoon ground ginger

Put the tamarind pulp, jaggery and dates in a pan along with 300ml (½ pint) water. Bring to the boil, then cook over a low heat for 25–30 minutes until all the pulp has softened and the chutney looks thick and gloopy.

Pass the mixture through a sturdy sieve set over a bowl. This will take a few minutes, as you will have to press the mixture firmly through the sieve so that you get all the pulp but leave behind the tamarind seeds and other bits.

Transfer the mixture back to the pan and bring to the boil, then add the cumin and ginger along with ¼ teaspoon salt and ¼ teaspoon chilli powder. Mix well and let it cool completely before using or decanting to a sterilized jar.

This easy, fresh coconut chutney works a treat with any snack and goes perfectly with South Indian food, such as Lemon Rice (see page 144) or Rice Pancakes (see page 173). But don't just stop there, enjoy this in wraps or with paratha (see pages 160–70) and pakora (see pages 22–7). Tinned coconut meat can be found in Asian supermarkets.

NARIYAL CHUTNEY
Coconut chutney

50g (1¾oz) peanuts, skin on

120g (4¼oz) fresh coconut meat

2 green chillies, stems removed

4 tablespoons natural yogurt

1 teaspoon black mustard seeds

Dry-roast the peanuts in a frying pan for 5 minutes over a low heat until they have changed colour. Set them aside to cool slightly.

In a blender, combine the cooled peanuts with the coconut meat, chillies and yogurt. Add ¼ teaspoon salt, ¼ teaspoon chilli powder and 4 tablespoons water. Blitz until smooth.

Heat 2 tablespoons oil in a small pan and add the mustard seeds. Once they start to sizzle, pour them over the chutney and serve.

COCONUT CHUTNEY

TAMARIND CHUTNEY

CORIANDER CHUTNEY

This is hands-down the chutney I make the most. It's the one I serve with any snack, dinner, starter or even just some crisps. Once you have tried it, it's a chutney you will want to make again and again. It takes just a few seconds to blitz and keeps in the refrigerator for 3–4 days. Fresh, fragrant, light, you can adjust the heat level to your taste.

DHANIYA CHUTNEY

Coriander chutney

30g (1oz) fresh coriander, leaves and stalks

10g (¼oz) fresh mint leaves

juice of 1 lemon

2 tablespoons natural yogurt

2 green chillies, stems removed (and deseeded, if wished)

In a food processor, blitz the coriander, mint, lemon juice, yogurt and chillies along with ½ teaspoon salt and ½ teaspoon sugar until smooth. Don't be tempted to add any water to this – let it blitz with just the ingredients above to achieve the right consistency.

A lovely cooling side dish to go with anything you make from this recipe book. Whether you choose a flatbread or a rice dish, some snacks or a curry, fish, chicken or veg, this raita will be a great accompaniment to them all.

KHERA RAITA
Cucumber yogurt

SERVES 4

1 whole cucumber, grated
300g (10½oz) natural yogurt
½ teaspoon ground cumin
1 green chilli, thinly sliced

Put the cucumber on a plate and sprinkle with ½ teaspoon salt. Let it sit for 15 minutes.

In a bowl, mix the yogurt with ½ teaspoon chilli powder, ½ teaspoon sugar and the ground cumin.

Squeeze the excess moisture from the cucumber and add the flesh to the yogurt and mix well. Sprinkle the chillies on top and serve.

This is a great dish that you can enjoy on its own or as a side to a curry or *sabji*. I like to have some form of raita with all my meals, whether I make it fresh or prepare it beforehand and serve it chilled. The mustard seeds and curry leaves make this so flavourful.

ALU RAITA

Potato yogurt

SERVES 4

1 potato, peeled and cut into
  1-cm (½-inch) cubes
300g (10½oz) natural yogurt
1 teaspoon ground cumin
1 teaspoon black mustard
  seeds
10–12 curry leaves

Cook the potato cubes in a pan of boiling water until soft, then drain and leave to cool.

In a large bowl, combine the yogurt with 200ml (7fl oz) water along with ½ teaspoon salt, ½ teaspoon chilli powder and the ground cumin. Add the cooled potatoes to the mixture and mix well.

Heat 2 tablespoons oil in a small pan and add the mustard seeds. Once they start to pop, remove from the heat and add the curry leaves. Pour this over the raita and serve.

Honestly, I could eat this just as it is, on its own – that's how amazing this tastes. Still, it is one incredible side dish to enjoy with a whole meal or with some *pulao*, paratha (see pages 160–70) or a warm roti (see page 159) with ghee.

BAIGAN RAITA
Aubergine yogurt

SERVES 4

2 aubergines, cut into 1-cm (½-inch) cubes

200g (7oz) Greek yogurt

1 teaspoon ground cumin

handful of fresh coriander, leaves roughly torn

handful of pomegranate seeds

Put the aubergine pieces on a plate and sprinkle 1 teaspoon of salt over the top. Let it sit for 30 minutes–1 hour, then pat the aubergines dry.

Heat enough oil for shallow-frying in a large, deep frying pan. Fry the aubergine pieces until beautifully golden, then remove from the pan to drain on some kitchen paper.

Mix the yogurt with ½ teaspoon salt, ½ teaspoon chilli powder and ½ teaspoon of the ground cumin.

Spread the yogurt over a shallow serving bowl, top with the fried aubergine pieces and then sprinkle with the rest of the ground cumin, the coriander and pomegranate seeds. Serve.

This is a very popular raita that is made with *boondi*, which is made from a gram-flour batter that has been fried into tiny balls. You can buy these ready-made in packs from Asian supermarkets. Once added to the yogurt, the crispy balls soak it up and become soft and delicious. You can prepare this a few hours before serving and let it chill in the refrigerator.

BOONDI RAITA
Gram-flour balls in yogurt

SERVES 4

300g (10½oz) natural yogurt

1 teaspoon ground cumin

70g (2½oz) boondi (gram-flour balls)

10–12 fresh mint leaves, finely chopped, plus extra for serving

handful of pomegranate seeds

In a large bowl, mix the yogurt with 100ml (3½fl oz) water, ½ teaspoon salt, ½ teaspoon chilli powder and the ground cumin. Add the boondi and let it sit for 10 minutes to soften.

Add the mint and mix well. Sprinkle with the pomegranate seeds, a pinch of chilli powder and extra mint leaves, and serve.

MORE WAYS WITH

RAITA

Raita (yogurt dishes) make an ideal cooling side to Indian curries and snacks. I also love them for dipping flatbread into or on the side of a rice dish. There are so many ways of adding interest. Vegetables add a bit of crunchy texture – I've already shown in this chapter delicious options for potato and aubergine, but most salad vegetables are ideal, chopped up finely and simply stirred through. The only thing to avoid is adding too much moisture, so ensure you squeeze wet vegetables until dry or discard any watery, pulpy seeds. Spicing can be varied to suit your taste: an extra pinch of cumin or ground coriander here, some extra hot chillies there – you can really play around and have fun.

For a refreshing **onion raita**, replace the boondi with 2 finely chopped onions and swap the mint for a handful of finely chopped fresh coriander and 1 thinly sliced red chilli.

For a **tomato raita**, use 2 tomatoes instead, discarding the pulp and chopping the flesh into small pieces. Swap the mint for a handful of finely chopped fresh coriander.

A great crunchy fresh salad to go on your dinner table with a lovely dal rice or some paratha (see pages 160–70), some *sabji*, or just on its own, because why not?!

Crunchy salad

SERVES 4

½ cucumber, cut into small cubes

2 tomatoes, cut into small cubes

1 red onion, cut into small cubes

2 tablespoons lemon juice

½ teaspoon Chaat Masala (see page 13)

Put the cucumber, tomatoes and onion in a bowl and mix well.

In a separate bowl, whisk the lemon juice with 2 tablespoons olive oil, ¼ teaspoon salt, ¼ teaspoon black pepper and the chaat masala.

Pour the dressing over the salad, mix well and serve.

This salad may seem simple, but the flavour is sharp and peppery from the rocket leaves and the yogurt tempered with spices brings it to life. It's a great little salad to eat along with some barbecued meats or a simple dal and rice. I also enjoy this with some slices of sourdough.

ALU SALAD
Potato salad

SERVES 4

500g (1lb 2oz) baby potatoes

1 teaspoon black mustard seeds

15–20 fresh curry leaves, half chopped, half left whole

150g (5½oz) Greek yogurt

100g (3½oz) rocket leaves

Cut the potatoes in half and put them in a saucepan of cold water. Bring the water to the boil and cook the potatoes for 10–12 minutes until cooked through. Drain and set aside to cool to lukewarm.

Heat 2 tablespoons ghee or oil in a frying pan and add the mustard seeds. Once they start to pop, add the curry leaves, then take it off the heat. Add 1 teaspoon salt and 1 teaspoon chilli powder and mix well. Pour the spice mix into the yogurt and mix well. Pour the tempered yogurt over the potatoes and mix again.

You have the option of serving the potato salad on top of a bed of rocket leaves or you can mix the leaves directly into the potatoes. I prefer to mix it all together, but it tastes great either way.

You just need a big spoon and a sunny spot to sit and enjoy this delicious salad. The sourness of the mangoes goes perfectly with the crunch of the onions and the peanuts. This is a simple salad that you can prepare using the very green, raw mangoes that you can usually find in the supermarkets. It's great with any meal that you might be planning to cook.

AAM SALAD

Mango salad

SERVES 4

50g (1¾oz) peanuts, skin on

2 raw mangoes, cut into 5-mm (¼-inch) cubes

1 red onion, cut into 5-mm (¼-inch) cubes

1 teaspoon black mustard seeds

10–12 curry leaves

Dry-roast the peanuts in a frying pan for 5 minutes over a low heat, stirring through until roasted and aromatic. Crush them roughly in a pestle and mortar so that all the nuts have broken up.

Put the mangoes and onions in a bowl along with the crushed peanuts.

Heat 2 tablespoons oil or ghee in a small pan and add the mustard seeds. Once they start to pop, remove from the heat and add the curry leaves, ¼ teaspoon salt and ¼ teaspoon chilli powder. Pour this over the salad and give it a good mix before serving.

SWEET

My mum has been making many variations of the simple *atta laddoo* for years. You can try out different combinations of nuts for these *laddoos* – instead of walnuts, try almonds or cashews, or even a mixture. The roasting of the *atta* (chapatti flour) is key though, as it adds to the flavour with the aromatic cardamom. These *laddoo* are so delicious and nutritious and will keep well in an airtight box for a good couple of weeks.

ATTA LADDOO

Wholemeal laddoo

MAKES 12

60g (2¼oz) walnuts

150g (5½oz) chapatti flour (atta)

3 tablespoons almond butter

5 tablespoons agave syrup

seeds of 4–5 green cardamom pods, crushed to a powder

In a hot pan, dry-roast the walnuts for 3–4 minutes. Let cool, then transfer to a pestle and mortar or small food processor and crush to a fine powder. Transfer to a bowl.

In the same pan, dry-roast the chapatti flour for 10 minutes over a low heat, stirring frequently. Once it starts to change colour and become aromatic, add 50g (1¾oz) ghee. Mix well, then transfer it to the bowl with the walnut powder.

Add the almond butter, agave syrup and ground cardamom seeds to the bowl and mix it all well. Shape the mixture into walnut-sized balls and enjoy.

This is one of my favourite desserts. Although *kheer* can be made with different things, rice *kheer* is my favourite. It's creamy, wholesome and delicious with just a gentle sweetness. The best part is that you can enjoy this nice and warm or prepare it ahead of time and enjoy it chilled. Top with pistachios, as here, or use a mix of nuts, such as cashews or almonds, and raisins too.

KESAR KHEER

Saffron rice pudding

SERVES 4

80g (3oz) basmati rice

1 litre (1¾ pints) whole milk

2 pinches of saffron

seeds of 4–6 green cardamom pods, crushed to a powder

handful of pistachios, roughly chopped

Soak the rice in water for 30 minutes, then drain well. Transfer the rice to a pestle and mortar and crush it to break up the grains.

Heat the milk in a large pan and bring to the boil. Add the saffron and then the rice and cook over a low heat for 30–35 minutes until the rice is cooked and mushy.

Add the crushed cardamom seeds along with 50g (1¾oz) sugar to the pan and mix well. Cook over a low heat for 5 minutes until the kheer thickens and the sugar has dissolved.

Sprinkle the pistachios on top and serve.

MORE
WAYS
WITH

KHEER

This rice *kheer* is a wonderfully adaptable recipe. I love a simple
saffron rice pudding, but omit the saffron and you have a versatile,
creamy, gently sweet dessert that lends itself to all sorts of different
toppings of fresh or dried fruits, nuts, spices and even chocolate.
Cloves, cinnamon, vanilla and flower waters all make
lovely additions.

To make a **mango kheer**, leave out the saffron from the kheer
base. Thinly chop the flesh of 2 ripe mangoes and arrange prettily
on top of the kheer along with the pistachios.

For a decadent **chocolate kheer**, omit the saffron. Roughly chop
25g (1oz) dark chocolate (70% cocoa solids) and place in a bowl.
Heat 50ml (2fl oz) double cream in a small pan until just boiling,
then pour it over the chocolate in the bowl and mix to a lovely
shiny ganache. Pour half of the ganache over the kheer. Don't
mix it in fully, just swirl it a few times. Spoon into bowls and
drizzle the remaining ganache on top. Serve warm.

These are little treats that I make every Diwali for my family and friends. They are one of the quickest Indian sweets to make and they disappear even quicker – a must-try if you have a sweet tooth.

NARIYAL LADDOO
Coconut laddoo

MAKES ABOUT 10

100g (3½oz) desiccated coconut

seeds of 4–5 green cardamom pods

200ml (7fl oz) condensed milk

a handful of pistachios, crushed to a fine powder

Dry-roast the coconut in a frying pan over a low heat for 2–3 minutes until it starts to change colour and become aromatic.

Crush the cardamom seeds in a pestle and mortar and add them to the coconut, then add the condensed milk to the pan and continue to cook over a low heat. Keep stirring for 2–3 minutes until the mixture comes together and starts to leave the sides of the pan. Remove from the heat and let it cool slightly for 5 minutes.

While still warm, divide the mixture into about 10 small portions and roll each into a ball shape. Roll the balls in the pistachio powder, covering them well. Let them cool completely, then enjoy.

Growing up, this was one of my favourite sweets that my mum made at home. Most of our Indian sweets were store-bought, but there were some things that were always made at home, such as this *halwa*. Whether it was made for a festival or a wedding or another special occasion, this *halwa* would be made with plenty of ghee and enjoyed by all. If you have any left over, store it in the refrigerator, but always remember to warm it up before eating to get that ghee melted and tasting delicious.

SOOJI HALWA

Semolina halwa

SERVES 4-6

120g (4¼oz) semolina

seeds of 4–5 green cardamom pods, crushed to a powder

20g (¾oz) cashews, thinly sliced

20g (¾oz) almonds, thinly sliced

20g (¾oz) raisins, thinly sliced

Dry-roast the semolina in a saucepan over a low heat for 5 minutes until it changes colour and becomes golden. Add 100g (3½oz) ghee to the semolina and cook for another 5 minutes over a low heat until it turns a caramel colour.

Meanwhile, in a separate pan, combine 440ml (15½fl oz) water and 80g (2¾oz) sugar with the cardamom powder and cook until the sugar has dissolved.

In another small pan, heat 2 tablespoons ghee. Add the nuts and raisins and cook for 2 minutes until they start to change colour. Set aside.

Slowly add the sugar water to the semolina pan while stirring continuously. Cook for 1–2 minutes until all the liquid has been absorbed by the semolina.

Sprinkle the semolina with the fried raisins and nuts, then serve.

A delicious sweet that tastes fragrant and feels light as air. The saffron adds a gentle touch to this spongy little delicacy.

Rasgulla

MAKES 12

1 litre (1¾ pints) whole milk
pinch of saffron
juice of 1 lemon
1 tablespoon cornflour

Put the milk in a saucepan, add the saffron and bring to the boil. Add the lemon juice and mix well, then remove from the heat and set aside for 5 minutes.

Line a sieve with a muslin cloth, then strain the mixture over a bowl or the sink. This will collect all the milk fats (solids) and drain the whey. Gather the cloth at the top and twist to get rid of all the excess liquid. Put a couple of cans or a heavy pestle on top of the muslin while it sits on the sieve and leave it like that for 10 minutes.

Put 200g (7oz) sugar and 700ml (1¼ pints) water in a separate saucepan and bring to the boil. Turn the heat off once the sugar has dissolved.

Take the milk solids from the muslin and place on a clean surface. Sprinkle the cornflour on top and start kneading with the palm of your hand. It will start as a crumbly mix, but continue to knead for 5 minutes and the mixture will come together into a smooth, soft dough. Divide the dough into 12 portions and shape each into a smooth ball.

Slowly add the balls to the hot sugar syrup, cover and cook over a low heat for 15 minutes until the balls have doubled in size and are soft and spongy. You might have to do this in batches.

Serve them in a little syrup and enjoy warm or chilled.

Chaas is a very refreshing spiced drink served in the summer to cool you down. It's also served with meals in hot weather to help digest the food. This is usually made with a bit of fresh chilli, but you can leave that out and just add ¼ teaspoon chilli powder instead. That gentle heat from the chilli along with cumin and mint makes it super delicious. You can make this a few hours in advance and let it chill in the refrigerator.

CHAAS

Buttermilk

SERVES 2

100g (3½oz) natural yogurt

¼ teaspoon ground cumin

1 teaspoon finely chopped fresh root ginger

10 fresh mint leaves

1 small green chilli, finely chopped

Put the yogurt in a little jug, add the cumin along with ¼ teaspoon salt and whisk to combine well.

Put the chopped ginger, mint leaves and chilli in a pestle and mortar and crush thoroughly. Add this to the spiced yogurt and stir it in.

Finally, add around 300ml (10fl oz) water and combine it well. Serve with or without ice.

This hot drink is perfect all year round. Helping you stay warm in the winter or keeping you cool in the summer, masala chai will be offered to you when you enter any Indian's home as a welcome drink. It is also served as an after-meal digestive. It's a warm hug in a bowl! For perfect results, use Assam or Darjeeling tea leaves and let it brew a little once it boils. It works best with whole dairy milk and not milk alternatives. To make it dairy-free, skip other milk options completely and have it black.

Masala chai

SERVES 2

1-cm (½-inch) piece of fresh root ginger

2 green cardamom pods

4 cloves

1 tablespoon loose tea leaves (preferably Assam)

50ml (2fl oz) whole milk

Put 300ml (10fl oz) water in a small pan. Smash the ginger and cardamom pods in a pestle and mortar, just to open them up a little, and add to the water along with the cloves, tea leaves and 1 tablespoon sugar.

Bring to the boil, then add the milk and bring back to the boil. Let it simmer over a low heat for 2 minutes before straining. Serve immediately.

Index

UK/US terms

aubergine – eggplant

baking tray – baking sheet

barbecue – grill

beetroot/s – beet/s

butter beans – lima beans

caster sugar – superfine sugar

chestnut mushrooms – cremini mushrooms

chickpeas – garbanzo beans

chilli/chillies – chili/chiles

chilli flakes – red pepper flakes

coriander (fresh) – cilantro

cornflour – cornstarch

crisps – chips

desiccated coconut – dried unsweetened shredded coconut

double cream – heavy cream

frying pan – skillet

grill – broil/broiler

haricot beans – navy beans

kitchen foil – aluminum foil

kitchen paper – paper towels

muslin – cheesecloth

natural yogurt – plain yogurt

peanut oil – groundnut oil

plain flour – all-purpose flour

prawn – shrimp

rapeseed oil – canola oil

roasting tin – roasting pan

rocket – arugula

sieve – strainer

starter – appetizer

tomato purée – tomato paste

whole milk – full-fat milk

wholemeal – wholewheat

Acknowledgements

This book needed a big push to make it happen. I was looking for that perfect subject matter to bite into, and for that I must thank Publisher Kate Fox, for helping me figure out this puzzle and for her guidance throughout the writing of this book.

As always, it can only happen with an amazing team, which I am very lucky to have. Big thanks to the Art Director Juliette Norsworthy, who after working on nine books together gets it before I even say anything. Thanks to Senior Editor Leanne Bryan, who keeps me in check and does not let a thing go amiss. Thanks also to the wonderful Production Manager Caroline Alberti, for making the photos look so gorgeous. A big thanks to the rest of the team at Octopus for all your hard work.

Many thanks to the lovely Nassima Rothacker, who has not only photographed every single book of mine, but is also genuinely the loveliest person to work with. She brings the recipes to life in a way only she can.

Thanks to the food stylist Maddie Rix, who really got under the skin of the book and recipes and made every single plate of food shine. Thanks to Lauren Miller for hunting down the perfect props for this mission. And thanks to Emily Preece-Morrison for her expert editing.

I could not finish this last part of the book without thanking my family. Visiting my parents just before I started writing this book reminded me why and how I am doing what I am doing. My mum and dad are such an inspiration – their positivity in life, their kindness and love is something I am very lucky to have received, and for that I am so grateful. Not forgetting their love for food and the strong sweet tooth that I have inherited from them.

Thanks to my husband Gaurav, who has never questioned but has endured all the recipe testing I inflict on him. Maybe 'endure' is not the right word, but he gets what I cook and has never once complained. He gives a good pep talk whenever I need one and is always my biggest cheerleader.

And finally, thank you my kids – Sia and Yuv – who really could not love and support me any more. How could I do anything without them? No, they don't actually do any washing up, but they are the most honest and best critics I could have. I hope all these books that I am writing will be used in their own homes one day!

About the author

Chetna Makan was born in Jabalpur in Central India. After rising to fame as one of the best-loved contestants on *The Great British Bake Off* in 2014, she has written nine cookbooks and has a highly engaged social media following, with over 1.1 million followers across her platforms.

www.chetnamakan.co.uk

chetnamakan

X chetnamakan

FoodwithChetna

chetna.makan